# Toddy to Tequila

# Todday to Tequila

## The Story of Alcohol in India

Sandhya Mulchandani

JUGGERNAUT BOOKS
C-I-128, First Floor, Sangam Vihar, Near Holi Chowk,
New Delhi 110080, India

First published by Juggernaut Books 2026



10 9 8 7 6 5 4 3 2 1

P-ISBN: 9789353456771
E-ISBN: 9789353453565



Typeset in Adobe Caslon Pro by R. Ajith Kumar, Noida

Printed at Thomson Press India Private Limited

Wine doesn't ask questions, wine understands –
Oftentimes better than people …

# Contents

# Introduction

At the outset, this is not a book about the processes involved in making alcohol, nor is it about what to or where to drink or what ensues after the drinking. It's not a book about mixing cocktails either. This is a book about the genesis of what you're drinking, the stories of where it came from and, though Indians have always been drinking, how drinking culture has evolved, with new layers added with every passing generation. Alcohol is more than a mere social habit in India; it forms a cultural continuum.

This is a book that traces the journey of alcohol through the centuries – how it has been celebrated and reviled, taxed and outlawed, hidden in earthen pots and flaunted in stone-studded gold and silver goblets … Every bottle tells a story, varied and subjective. In India, the narrative is as old as the Vedas and as new as the shiny bottles lining the flashy liquor shops in

Gurugram. It has permeated through every segment of society, from being consumed by the gods in Vaikunth and Kailash and offered in Vedic sacrifices, to being found in royal courts and battlefields, brewed in tribal huts and raucously debated in Parliament. It has variously been a sacred libation, a status symbol, an alluring temptation, an addiction as well as a very lucrative economic and political tool.

The book follows the evolution of alcohol through broad historical periods, beginning with the Vedic era and post-Vedic developments such as the introduction of taxes and licensing, and the emergence of Buddhism and Jainism, with the very first anti-alcohol doctrines. The writings of the renowned medical practitioners Charaka and Sushruta also introduced new lines of thought, including arguments for moderate alcohol use. The counterculture in the South during the same period, free from northern Brahmanical diktats, was of a more egalitarian society happily brewing alcohol from palm trees with no censure or restrictions.

Islamic influence changed the social fabric of India completely, its resplendent courts and kings exhibiting a complex interplay of widespread use of liquor and drugs set amidst the clear Quranic opposition to alcohol consumption. The fragmentation of the Mughal

Empire saw the rise of western seafaring nations, again deeply influencing Indian lives.

So, the narrative about alcohol reflects these shifts in power, trade, faith and class. It reveals hierarchies of purity and pollution, caste and gender restrictions and the tug of war between pleasure and prohibition.

Myths, contradictions and duplicity abound about the genesis of alcohol, inebriated gods and the first men who discovered and brewed it, and continue to influence more contemporary and sanctimonious beliefs, like the idea that Indians never drank in the past and that it was a habit brought in by foreigners. Unlike in East Asia or Europe, where alcohol developed in a fairly linear tradition, in India, it's a patchwork of ritual, medicine, community, tradition and colonialism.

But ultimately, it's about people – the people who first made, drank, enjoyed and abused it; the people who became wealthy from it, who fought and even murdered for it. It's about the gods who first created it, the sages who elevated it to the status of divinity, the kings who imposed taxes on it to generate revenue, the soldiers who drank it for Dutch courage before battle, the men who drank it in company, the women who distilled it. The abstainers and naysayers, Muslim emperors and British corporals, saints and sinners – everyone has played a role in the drama that is alcohol, which has gotten intrinsically woven into the history, religious life and mythologies of India.

From being a land that celebrated its Soma to, many centuries later, once again rising as a producer of some of the world's best spirits, India has come full circle. It's been a saga of turbulence, excesses, resistance and reinvention – nonetheless, its very own narrative.

This, then, is the story of India and a story of alcohol that's flowed closely alongside India's history, reflecting its culture and ambiguities, its excesses, exuberance and travails.

# 1

# Euphoric Beginnings: Soma and Sura

The first thought to have arisen in the Primeval Being was one of desire. Thus, desire in Indian mythology is considered to be an innate element that makes up human beings – be it for material goods, spirituality, relationships, food or drink.

Seen as a fundamental human necessity, all aspects of desire were enthusiastically embraced, alcohol amongst them. Described as something that brought about exuberance, tolerance, happiness and valour, besides altering the mind and intellect, Soma, the first brew, was considered to be sentient – a living entity; therefore, blessed by the gods. So, much like these gods, Sura and Soma too developed their own mythologies and occupy an exalted position in the Vedic texts.

The Vedic period is loosely dated between 1500 and 800 BCE, years that saw the advent of the Aryans, Sanskrit, the Vedas and an organized religion that was the precursor to Hinduism as we know it today. However, it also brought with it caste divisions, social hierarchies as well as wealth disparities that were codified in books like the Puranic epics, the Grha Sutras, the Manusmriti and the Arthashastra.

India is a glorious country, colourful and ebullient, stoic in the face of insurmountable difficulties, but a place where life is celebrated as an *utsav*, a carnival. There are no disinterested bystanders in India; rather, every man, woman and child is an enthusiastic and willing participant in this exuberance that we call life.

And it has always been so. From the very beginning of civilization, when men hunted and huddled together, pondering life under august moons and starlit skies, the quest was to find meaning, both metaphysical and physical, which was interpreted as seeking happiness, pleasure and peace. The first settlements in the subcontinent embodied just this.

Excavations of the Indus Valley townships showcase not just a politically and architecturally advanced civilization, but also a socially adept one with high culture. It is amply clear that 5,000 years ago, people took pleasure just as seriously as they did work. While the script and the numerous clay tablets of Harappa have yet to be deciphered, there can be no ambiguity about what the large fermentation vats found at the sites were used for, making the Indian subcontinent probably one of the first few regions in the world where alcohol was brewed. Much like in Pompeii but almost 1,500 years earlier, there is evidence of large distillation pits and even seating arrangements for regular clients in taverns and brothels.

And it continued to flourish, until the entire civilization mysteriously collapsed.

---

When the peripatetic, pastoral Aryan settlers came from Central Asia, they brought with them cattle, horses and, amongst other things, their rudimentary language and an interesting array of gods. With borrowed elements from Central Asia, Bactria and Margiana, these eclectic gods soon got assimilated into the existing beliefs and practices that prevailed in the Indus Valley. There was nothing subtle or subdued about these gods; they were primeval beings – temperamental, energetic and dynamic representations of natural elements like rain and thunder, fire, earth, and water. To appease these uncontrollable forces of nature, the Aryans composed a large body of verse in Sanskrit that sang their praise and placated their egos with sacrifices to ensure their continued grace. These collective verses, called the Vedas, form the largest extant body of scriptural works in the world.

These verses, besides containing hymns to a number of gods like Varuna, the god of rain, and Agni, the god of fire, also propitiate Usas, the goddess of dawn; they also sing paeans of praise to Soma, a plant that is variously taken to be a hallucinogen, an opiate and manna from heaven. Probably used by them to dispel fatigue and restore energy and well-being, Soma's uses and effects were well known to the early settlers.

Though the people of the Indus Valley – and the Chinese even before them – had perfected the art of brewing liquor, the first mention of a powerful sap appears in the Rg Veda (c. 1700 BCE), which extols the virtues of Soma. The Zoroastrians of Persia had a similar plant sap that they called haoma, but Soma attained cult status in South Asia. This was no ordinary plant secretion; its effect on the human mind was so expansive that it immediately inspired souls to take flight, made their imaginations soar and made them sexually potent and invincible – almost godlike.

It made a hard life look so very good and worthwhile.

There are ongoing debates that claim Soma was more opioid than liquor. Ancient texts describe the plant variously as a sap, a fermented drink or a spirit, but settle the debate by calling it the 'drink of the gods'. Stupefied by the near magical effects of Soma, sages with an interest in the nature of god or the ultimate reality saw it as a direct gift from the heavens that helped their minds breach boundaries and experience the vastness as well as the oneness of the universe. These expansive experiences helped turn Soma into something sacred, to be cherished and imbibed as a sacrament. It, thus, attained an elevated status – consecrated, its consumption initially restricted to the 'seekers': saints, seers and holy men.

---

Described as having yellow drooping boughs with knotty joints, Soma exuded an abundance of milky sap, which was tapped by moonlight along the Himalayan mountaintops and mixed with other ingredients to produce the intoxicating beverage. Although initially the drink was mainly associated with spiritual activities, it soon became just that – a drink on which much time, effort and research was conducted to produce the best liquor. The celestial sage Narada says in the Narada Purana (III.90.11), 'This Vidya is as exhilarating as the intoxicating liquor. It is the means of overcoming distress. I shall now tell you the precise preparation of it.'[1]

So, especially in the course of yagnas, it was prepared with great ceremony, pressed between stones amidst chants of Vedic shlokas and incantations, mixed with milk, strained and offered as prasad and oblation.

Ancient sages deified what, to them, were incomprehensible mysteries, like conception, or how a few drops of plant sap could have such a dramatic effect on human beings. And so mythic tales were born. Soma has several narratives about its genesis that appear in the Rg Veda, the Puranas and the Brahmanas, amongst others. According to one version of the story, the Soma plant was supposed to have been in the possession of the Gandharvas (residents of the present-day Afghanistan–Pakistan border), zealously guarded by an archer named Krishanu, probably their king. A falcon called Suparna was sent to steal the plant. He is said to have flown high up to the third heavens where, as per the Rg Veda (VIII.82.9), it was kept guarded within an iron fort. When Krishanu saw the falcon carry away Soma, he shot the bird, who lost its wings and dropped the Soma to the earth.

> The straight-flying hawk, conveying the Soma plant from afar; the bird attended by the gods, brought, resolute of purpose, the adorable, exhilarating Soma, having taken it from the lofty heaven. (Rg Veda [4.26.6])[2]

In another version, the king of the gods, Lord Indra, went out in the guise of a ram and stole Soma. More risqué tales appear later in texts like the Taittiriya Samhita and the Aitreya Brahmana, in which the devas want to steal it from the Gandharvas but can't come up with a viable plan. Knowing the Gandharvas' fondness for women, they decide to barter a woman for it, but again can't find a woman who would consent to the plan. Finally, Vac (the goddess of speech and knowledge), assuming the form of a beautiful woman, is traded for Soma Rasa. The tale reiterates the high esteem in which Soma was held.

> Speech said, 'The Gandharvas love women; with me as a woman do ye barter it.' 'No,' replied the gods, 'how could we be without you?' She replied, 'Still

do ye buy; when ye will have need of me, then shall I return to you.' 'Be it so' (they replied). With her as a great naked one they bought Soma… (Aitreya Brahmana [1.5.27])[3]

Soma became such an integral part of the Vedic ritual that the sages wrote several hymns in its praise and created a separate chapter or mandala in its honour; there are more than 114 hymns dedicated exclusively to it in the Rg Veda. It became a special god to whom the Brahmin priests prayed for grace, largess and plenitude.

Well-skilled in speech we magnify thee, Soma, with our sacred songs:
Come thou to us, most gracious One. (Rg Veda [1.91.11])

Enricher, healer of disease, wealth-finder, prospering our store, Be, Soma, a good Friend to us. (Rg Veda [1.90.12])

Invincible in fight, saver in battles, guard of our camp, winner of light and water, Born amid hymns, well-housed, exceeding famous, victor, in thee will we rejoice, O Soma. (Rg Veda [1.90.21])[4]

The king of the gods was Indra. The ruler of the heavens, lightning, thunder, storms, rains and rivers, and one of the first gods to be mentioned in the Rg Veda, Indra has the largest number of verses, some 250 of them, dedicated to him. He is the god of war, wielder of Vajra the thunderbolt, and is usually described rather unfavourably as being rowdy, rancorous, adulterous and potbellied from excessive drinking. His wife, Indrani, taunts him for being an alcoholic, inept and overweight. She chides him to do his duties as the king of gods and even threatens to run off with a more suitable and handsome god if he doesn't shape up. Indrani's threats notwithstanding, Indra continues his drinking and womanizing.

> Narayana said [to Narada]:– In ancient days, Indra the Lord of the three worlds, intoxicated with wine and becoming lustful and shameless, began to enjoy Rambha in a lonely grove. (Devi Bhagavata Purana [9.40.13–25])[5]

Given to many a misadventure usually triggered by Soma, Indra is not known for his restraint or moderation and is only saved by the helpful twins called the Ashvins, gods associated with medicine and health, who are always at hand to administer an antidote for his hangovers and restore him to his senses.

The Rg Veda eulogizes Indra as the Deva Samrat (the king of the gods), the dragon slayer, a fearless warrior and an enthusiastic imbiber of Soma.

> His belly, drinking deepest draughts of Soma, like an ocean swells. (Rg Veda [1.7.7])
>
> Come Indra and delight thee with the juice at all the Soma feasts. (Rg Veda [1.9.1])
>
> Indra and Soma burn, destroy the demon foe, send downwards, O ye Bulls, those who add gloom to gloom. (Rg Veda [7.104.1])[6]

The best-known tale in the Rg Veda about Indra is how excessive Soma made him so insolent and arrogant that he even became disrespectful to his guru Brihaspati, who, on being thus insulted, withdrew support from the devas who were then at war with the asuras. Soon realizing that they had no guru, the devas sought the help of Lord Brahma, who recommended Vishwarupa. Always sceptical of Vishwarupa's allegiance, Indra one day heard him praying for the welfare of the asuras, flew into a rage and killed him.

When Vishwarupa's father Tvashta learnt of his son's death, he created Trisiras (the three-headed one) to dethrone Indra. The three heads were called Somapitha, Surapitha and Annada, consumers of Soma, Sura and food, respectively. Fierce battles ensured, but eventually Indra managed to kill him too. Tvasta then conducted a yagna from which rose Vritra, one of the most powerful demons ever created. The ensuing battle between Vritra and Indra was long and hard, and finally, with a special weapon fashioned out of the bones of a sage called Dadhichi, Indra managed to kill the demon-dragon, but only after drinking three tankards of Soma. The imagery of Indra fighting the dragon after consuming Soma is very eloquently described in the Vedas:

> Impetuous as a bull, [Indra] chose Soma and in three sacred beakers drank the juices, Maghavan then grasped the thunder for his weapon and smote to death the firstborn of the dragons. (Rg Veda [1.32.3])[7]

Not that Indra was going to rest quietly on his laurels – he bragged loud and long not only about killing the dragon but also about his capacity to drink Soma and the powers it gives him:

Like wild winds
The draughts have raised me up.
Have I been drinking Soma? (Rg Veda [X.119.2])

The draughts have borne me up
As swift steeds a chariot.
Have I been drinking Soma? (Rg Veda [X.119.3])

The heavens above
Do not equal one half of me.
Have I been drinking Soma? (Rg Veda [X.119.7])

I will pick up the earth
And put it here or put it there
Have I been drinking Soma? (Rg Veda [X.119.9])[8]

Indra was not the only god addicted to Soma. There are several other deities as well as sages; pride of place amongst them goes to Agni, the god of fire. The discovery of fire is what set humans apart from animals – the magical quality of fire, its heat, warmth and light were considered to be a divine gift from God.

The Rg Veda venerates the effulgent Agni in over 200 hymns. Seen as a protector of men and their homes, Agni presides over all sacraments, witness to all that is sacred. As the Soma yagnas were central to Vedic worship, Agni became the primary recipient of the main oblation offered, which was Soma.

> Agni, taste this prepared oblation; accept it, Mighty One, and let it please you. Vouchsafe us good protection and kind favour: Grant to the sacrificer health and riches. (Rg Veda [1.93.7])

> Agni and Soma, cherish well our horses, and let our cows be fat who yield oblations. Grant power to us and to our wealthy patrons, and cause our holy rites to be successful. (Rg Veda [1.93.12])[9]

The love of Soma was not restricted to gods – after all, the people who partook most of the Soma during yagnas were the priests and sages. Dattatreya, the son of the great sage Atri and a great yogi himself, was considered to be one such serious imbiber of alcohol. In the Markandeya and Padma Puranas, when the gods facing defeat by the asuras in battle sought the assistance of Brihaspati, they were directed to

Dattatreya, who declines to help, saying, 'I am drinking strong drink, I have remnants of food in my mouth, nor have I subdued my senses. How is it, O gods, ye seek for victory over your enemies even from me?' (Markandeya Purana [18.23.32]).[10]

The Vedic vision of heaven as explained in the Atharva Veda is stated to be a land of *ananda* (bliss) that contains rivers of flowing wine. A later-day text describes heaven as being a place where:

> Those people of earthly world who had attained mastery over Lalita's Mantra attain the chamber of sapphire on giving up their bodies and stay there. They enjoy divine objects in the company of their womenfolk. They drink sweet wine and dance with great devotion. (Brahmanda Purana [4b.33.43–4])[11]

Thus, drinking essentially became a sacred duty. There was a ritual performed at the beginning of a famous yagna called the Vajapeya. This was the highest form of Soma Yagna involving the pressing of Soma and performed in autumn. The term 'Vajapeya' is a compound word, where *vaja* means the strengthening liquor and *peya* means that which is to be drunk. This was performed for 17 days; the yagna observed 17 *strotras* and 17 *shastras*. 'Five cups of Soma were offered to Indra as well as an additional 17 cups of Soma and 17 cups of Sura' to a whole host of other deities.[12]

Although used as a synonym for an intoxicant or drug, 'Soma' has multiple meanings. There are several references in the Vedas that clearly establish Soma as a gift from Ishvara; the ensuing intoxication meant giving up of one's individuality and a complete surrender to divine powers. Thus, it was used by the sages as something that made them 'see', something that expanded their minds so they could personally experience the oneness of the universe and eventually achieve a state of enlightenment.

> O Soma, being purified, bring us from all sides, for thou canst-riches and food with hero sons. (Rg Veda [5.61.6])

> Soma, pour blessings on our kine, pour forth the food that streams with milk. Increase the sea that merits laud. (Rg Veda [5.61.15])

> Chasing our foemen, driving off the godless, Soma floweth on, Going to Indra's special place. (Rg Veda [5.61.25])

> O Pavamana, hither bring great riches and destroy our foes. O Indu grant heroic fame. (Rg Veda [5.61.26])[13]

---

Of course, teetotalism, abstinence and moderation were entirely unknown to both the Vedic gods and sages.

According to legend, it was the overindulgence of Soma by the gods and sages that led to the creation of Sura as an antidote by the celestial physicians the Ashvins. A more likely explanation is that probably due to enthusiastic overuse, and despite its supernatural qualities, the supply of Soma began to dry up. The best Soma plants were grown in the shadows of the Hindu Kush mountains called Mujavat in present-day Afghanistan, which is said to supply 90 per cent of the world's opium. This region has always straddled trade routes between China, Central Asia, Greece and mainland Europe, and in all likelihood, Soma became a much-traded commodity. As the new settlements along the Indo-Gangetic plains were not conducive to cultivate the plant, Soma had to be purchased from these travelling traders, who then as now charged a hefty premium. Soon rendered unaffordable and scarce, it was replaced by a less potent alternative.

At any rate, the euphoria that Soma had generated soon lost its shine, due to either its high prices or adulteration or non-availability, and the sap soon metamorphosed into Soma the moon god, still libidinous and capable of inducing moon madness but without the ecstatic elation. But having experienced the elevated states induced by Soma, human beings were not going to give it up so easily.

The quest was now on for a substitute.

---

There is much debate on whether Sura was a beer, a distillate or an accidental drink fermented from leftover fruit. There is speculation on whether the early settlers grew enough rice and barley to actually make fermented drinks from grain. But what is evident is that whether by watching monkeys eating very ripe fruits off the trees and getting high or watching animals eating the fallen fruit off the ground and reaching a happy state there, the serious search on for a viable Soma replacement led to experimentation with fruits, grains and herbs, and Sura came into being.

Produced through fermentation and distillation, tried-and-tested processes that were already known from the time of the Harappans, Sura also finds mention in the Rg Veda as well as the Shukla Yajur Veda, which records it as being made from a variety of local produce, showing that the Aryans had by now turned into settled agriculturists.

—

Even though Sura was a distillate and man-made, like much else in Hindu mythology, the Vedas and Puranas also accorded Sura a divine birth, thereby giving it religious sanction. In a delicious twist of irony, the Indian god of wine is a woman called Varuni. Also known to be the wife of the Vedic god Varuna, Varuni is the goddess of liquor and intoxication. There are, as usual, conflicting narratives about Varuni's genesis. She is supposed to be one of several valuable items that emerged during the Samudra Manthan when the oceans were churned, along with Lakshmi, the goddess of wealth; Kamadhenu, the wishing cow; precious gems as well as Amrit, the nectar of immortality.

In an alternate narrative, in the Brahmanda Purana, Lalita Mahatmya (9.66–69):

When the ocean of Milk was churned by the Devas and Danavas, goddess Varuni with tremulous eyes on account of inebriety, rose up even as the Siddhas in the firmament began to think – 'What is this?' She smilingly stood in front of the Asuras.

The Daityas did not accept her. Therefore, and they became Asuras. They were given the appellation Asura in the sense 'Those who do not have *Sura* (liquor)'.[14]

The Ramayana too records:

Oh, Rama, the sons of Diti, namely asuraa-s, have not espoused that daughter of Rain-god, but oh, brave Rama, the sons of Aditi on their part, namely sura-s, have espoused that impeccable Vaaruni.

Thereby the sons of Diti are called asuraa-s, and the sons of Aditi are called suraa-s, and gods are delighted and rejoiced on espousing Vaaruni. (Ramayana 1.45.37–38)[15]

Varuni was given in marriage to Varuna, the god of rain, rivers and seas, and is represented in iconography as a goddess with four arms holding a cup of liquor, a bowl of cooked meat, a bejewelled jar and a blue lotus.

There is an important yagna called the Sautramani Yagna that is based around the myth about the effects of Soma on Indra and how the Ashvins cured him with Sura.

Once the process was set in motion, the ancients began to experiment with all kinds of produce and grew rather proficient in distilling alcohol. There are approximately 11 types of liquors mentioned in the scriptures, of which Sura, made from grains, was the most popular. Then there are others: As per Narada's claim mentioned earlier, the Narada Purana does give a detailed account of the various liquors available and their methods of preparation, claiming that the knowledge of making the liquor was as exhilarating as the intoxication induced by the alcohol:

> It is a means of overcoming distress. The liquor is classified into three types: Gaudi, made from jaggery, Paisti from fermented rice and Madhvi made from honey. Drinking these, the mind gets repose. Let it remain undisturbed for two days and it becomes tasty and auspicious, worthy of being offered for worship. This immediately becomes liquor which the gods are very fond of. (Narada Purana [3.90.11–22])[16]

If Vedic gods like Indra had been immersed in Soma, the later-day deities too were not far behind in their love for it.

---

The most prominent of the post-Vedic gods associated with alcohol is Siva, who is believed to first make his appearance in the Indus Valley seals as Pashupati. Whether this was indeed Siva or Rudra, whose name means 'the howler' or 'the wild one', is still debated, but Rudra eventually finds his way into the Rg Veda as a minor deity and has three hymns dedicated to him. Over time, as the Vedic gods changed, Rudra or Siva's role as a destroyer grows, finally becoming one of the Trinity. His appearance, too, undergoes change; he goes from being a handsome, strapping man to a dishevelled, half-naked deity covered in sack cloth and ashes, with snakes and tridents as accessories. Known to be partial to hallucinogens and liquor, Siva undergoes many a transformation depicting all of life's dichotomies and contradictions.

> You are a holder of the rod (of chastisement), the wielder of a staff, adorned with staff, and tonsured

> head. You are imbiber of poison, drinker of nectar, drinker of wine, drinker of milk and Soma juice. (Vayu Purana [1.30.265])
>
> O Siva, neither Brahma nor Visnu nor the ancient sages can understand your greatness precisely. (Vayu Purana [1.30.268])[17]

The one avatar of Siva that is closely associated with alcohol that has survived till the present day is that of Kala Bhairava. In the Siva Purana, the origin of Bhairava is attributed, to a debate between Brahma and Vishnu, where Brahma arrogantly claims to be the creator of the universe and the only one worthy of worship to the exclusion of both Vishnu and Siva. In an attempt to bring him down a notch or two, Siva creates Kala Bhairava, a fierce aspect of Siva who cuts off one of Brahma's five heads and thereby his ego. Brahma is, to this day, left with four heads.

Kala Bhairava represents time in all its vicissitudes and ensures awareness of life and death. He is a popular deity amongst followers of Tantra in which he is offered liquor as oblation, a practice that is followed even today in well-known Bhairava temples, where the deity miraculously drinks up all the alcohol that is offered to him. Moreover, Bhairava is also said to be the lord of directions and the *nagar kotwal* – the guardian of a town – in his case, the town being the city of Siva: Varanasi (previously Kashi). So, everyone entering the city had to pay obeisance to Kala Bhairava and make him an offering of a tot of alcohol.

This is a tradition that continues to this day in the city of Ujjain. The festival of Navratri culminates with a mystic annual event where the district collector of Ujjain places a bottle of local liquor on the lips of seven-foot-tall images of two sister goddesses, Mahamaya and Mahalaya, at the Chaubis Khamba Temple located in the shadow of the famous Mahakal Temple. The devis appear to drink up the liquor to the chanting and clapping of a large number of awestruck devotees who gather to witness the spectacle and receive a palmful of liquor as prasad.

This is followed by an equally intriguing day-long event called the Nagar Pooja, where a procession led by district collectorate officers, employees and chowkidars of nearby villages starts from the Chaubis Khambha Temple and covers over 40 temples of devis, Bhairavas and Hanumanji. At the head of the procession is a uniformed chowkidar holding an earthen pitcher containing liquor that trickles down on to the earth, uninterruptedly, throughout the 27-km-long journey.[18]

---

Soon the gods from the Vedas all but faded from memory, their place taken up by human avatars of gods, demigods and valiant kings. These representatives of gods and supermen were as serious about their liquor as their predecessors.

If Indra was the lord of liquor during Vedic times, by the Puranic period, the sobriquet had been passed on to Balarama, the older brother of Lord Krishna. Known variously as Balabhadra at the Jagannath Temple in Odisha, Halayudha, for his instrument of choice being a plough, and Sankarshana, the handsome one, Balarama remains an intriguing though underappreciated outlier in the Hindu pantheon. Tall and fair as his brother was dark, dressed in deep blue clothes and jewels and with the toddy palm tree as an emblem on his standard, there seems to be no hesitancy in the Puranic texts in calling him out for his drunken antics.

There's an oft-repeated story about the three siblings Jagannath (Krishna), Subhadra and Balarama, whose idols are taken out in a procession during the annual nine-day Rath Yatra festival in Puri. Traditionally, the Gajapathis, the kings of what is now Odisha, played a key role in the celebrations, serving as helpers to the Lord. Once, the story goes, while the idol of Balarama was being carried out of the sanctum, it slipped and fell. Alarmed at what seemed like a bad omen, the king declared it a calamitous event. Baneswar Vidyalankar, a renowned eighteenth-century scholar from Guptipara, in present-day West Bengal who was present when this mishap occurred, assuaged the king's worries, saying:

> My lord! It would be reasonable to deem it a bad omen if either Narayana (that is, Jagannath) or Subhadra had toppled; but it is only logical for the Plow-bearer, with his eyes rolling over in Kadamba induced stupor, to fall upon the ground! (Udbhata Chandrika [2.1.90])[19]

---

The earlier-mentioned Varuni is now also known as Kadambari, a name used for several alcoholic beverages, though it specifically stands for the fermented liquor from the flowers of the kadamba trees. This was the same sap that Balarama had once tasted on the banks of the Yamuna, and he is, therefore, feted as the discoverer of Kadambari. In direct contrast to his younger brother, Balarama is a simple, straight-speaking man, quick to anger but equally easy to please. Uninterested in Krishna's political machinations, he is usually portrayed with Varuni, both of them in a happy state, holding cups in their hands.

> Thereupon once on a time while separated from Krishna the powerful and beautiful Sangkarshana, ranging on the summit of the mountain, sat under a charming shade of a blossoming Kadamva tree, sweet-scented wind began to fan him. Thus served by the wind and smell of wine touching his nostril he felt a hankering for wine and his mouth began to dry up like one who had excessively drunk in the previous day. Thereupon recollecting the drinking of ambrosia in the days of yore, he, searching the wine, saw the Kadamva tree. Deposited in its cave, the water, that the clouds showered on the tree in the rains, had become a delightful wine. The powerful Baladeva was over-powered by thirst, so drinking that wine again and again, like a sick person drinking water he grew inebriete and his body began to reel. On account of his being drunk his eyes and face, resembling an

> autumnal moon, began to roll. The goddess Varuni, who was the churning rod of ambrosia unto the gods, was born in that Kadamva cave in the shape of wine. And so she passed by the name of Kadamvari. (Harivamsa Purana [2.41.5–13])[20]

---

Drinking was not the purview of male gods alone. Goddesses too were routinely appeased with offerings of liquor, meat and other sacrifices, chief amongst them being Kali, an aspect of Devi. Widely considered to be one of the most primeval forms to be worshipped, Devi represents fertility: The Mother Goddess and the creative energies of the universe date back to almost 10,000 years. The worship of this cult got refined during the era of the Indus Valley Civilization, only to get eclipsed by the very masculine Vedic gods and eventually re-emerge as the creative and feminine aspect of Siva. Here, ancient mythologies, pre-historic pagan practices, mythical cult worship and diverse female deities converge to become Devi and her various avatars who, like their male counterparts, are also appeased with offerings of wine and animal sacrifices:

> O goddess Durga, O destroyer of intractable distresses, O goddess destroying all evils (disasters), save me in all difficult situations. O Durga, I have sought refuge in you … After keeping awake that night, when the day has dawned, at the rise of Aruna, buffaloes and sheep should be beheaded in front. The animals may number a hundred, half of it (fifty) or half of half (twenty-five) as the devotee pleases. With potfull of *Sura* and *Asava* (liquor) the great goddess should be propitiated. The meat thereof should be given to Kapalikas as well as to servants and maidservants. (Skanda Purana [7.1.83.48–53])[21]

She is also known as Mahishasura Mardini, the killer of Mahishasura the Buffalo Demon, who had been granted a boon that no man could kill him, which made him invincible in the ongoing battle between the devas and asuras. Repeatedly defeated, the devas assembled in the mountains where their combined divine energies coalesced into Goddess Durga.

> The Daityas said:– 'O Lord, We have seen a grown up woman … The Devi is decorated with jewels and ornaments … She is not human or Asuri but Her form is extraordinary and beautiful. That noble lady

> is mounted on a lion, holding weapons on all Her eighteen hands and roaring loudly; She is drinking wine; so it seems that She is puffed up with liquor ... Sentiments of love, heroism, laughter, terror and wonder are all fully shining in Her; therefore we are much overpowered by the halo emitted from Her ... (Devi Bhagavata Purana [5.9.49–54])[22]

Like her Vedic counterpart Indra, Kali's battle with Mahishasura is also described in great detail in several texts.

> Going to the battle ground, the goddess Kali roared like a lion. On hearing that the Danavas fainted. She laughed boisterously again and again boding ill to the Asuras. She drank the distilled grape wine and danced on the battle ground. The manifestations of Durga viz – Ugradamstra (one with fierce fangs), Ugradanda (one with fierce baton) and Kotavi (the naked) danced on the battle ground and drank wine. (Shiva Purana [2.5.38.1–3])[23]

It was not just Kali who drank alcohol, other goddesses did too. Dhumavati and Chinnamasta, both Hindu deities and one of the 10 Mahavidyas or aspects of Devi, are both ferocious aspects of the goddess. Chinnamasta, the self-decapitated nude goddess, is usually found standing or seated on a divine copulating couple, holding her own severed head in one hand and a scimitar in the other. Dhumavati was depicted as an aged, ugly and restless widow with dishevelled hair and broken teeth, but her worship was considered a more advanced and esoteric practise. All of them are offered wine as oblation.

—

Shaktism is closely associated with Tantra, practices that often advocate the use of sacrifices, meats and liquor as part of the ritual. It is integral to the goddess's worship, especially amongst the Vamachara or left-hand Tantric sects, where wine, meat, ritual sex and fish constitute the *panch makara*s and are partaken of by the Tantric practitioner.

You might think these are archaic practices, but a 2016 *Hindustan Times* news report dated 17 April from Patiala reports, 'Administration officials said that [over a three-day period], as many as 25,000 bottles of liquor, 50 bucklings and 11 roosters were handed over to the administration after offerings by devotees. These offerings took place at the Kali temple in Patiala.'[24]

---

If the Vedic gods and goddesses lived joyously without inhibitions and restraints, the kings who followed in their wake emulated them. The epics Ramayana and Mahabharata are tales that centre around two avatars of Lord Vishnu. Gods, demigods, virtuous kings idolized as gods – whatever the reality, Rama and Krishna were acknowledged to have been born as Kshatriya kings. So, in what might seem unpalatable to the exponents of Hindutva today, there are several and oft-repeated instances of not just Rama partaking of alcohol but also his equally revered wife Sita, who is described as having a drink or two with her husband.

Kannada writer K.S. Bhagwan in his book *Rama Mandira Yake Beda* [Why a Ram Mandir Is Not Needed] quotes verses from Valmiki Ramayana that indicate that Lord Rama drank wine with his wife Sita, having returned to Ayodhya after many a misadventure. According to him, the couple Rama and Sita spend their evenings quietly enjoying wine and each other's company:

> All the trees in the forest were filled with flowers. And the rocks covered with falling flowers appeared like welkin beautified with stars. The garden was like Indra's Nandana and Kubera's Chitraratha made by Brahma. Having entered the rich forest Rama sat on a seat, covered with a beautiful coverlet and like Purandara with Saci he took Sita by the hand, made her sit by him and drink the wine distilled in the province of Mira.
>
> Taking Sita with both arms, he got her to taste the excellent maireyaka wine, like Indra to Saci would have given.[25]

This immediately sparked outrage amongst Hindu groups who rose in rebellion and strongly disagreed with Bhagwan's interpretation of these verses and offered counter arguments.

The preferred wine in Ayodhya appears to be maireyaka, which is a specific blend, often a combination of Sura and asava and prepared with various spices, jaggery, fruits and molasses. When Prince Bharat visits Rishi Bharadwaja, he hesitantly leaves behind his army, unsure how the sage could offer hospitality to so many people. Bharadwaja invokes Visvakarma (the architect of gods) in order to fulfil his duties towards the guests:

> I wish to offer hospitality to the guests, I summon Vishvakarma who is also the divine carpenter. Let arrangements be made for me. Let some rivers flow with Maireya, some others flow with highly refined spirituous liquor and some others flow with cool water with a taste of sugarcane. I invoke the fair women who are attending on Brahma the Lord of creation [...] May the blessed moon-god furnish me many-coloured flowers, drinks like wine and others as also various kinds of meat.[26] (Ramayana [2.91.12–21])

Sita, too, is said to have particularly enjoyed this variety of wine, which was usually served to guests at weddings and other ceremonies. It appears to have been a special drink, as Sita, when she proceeds to the forest with her husband, promises the river Ganga that she will propitiate her with a thousand pots of wine should they return unscathed. She said:

> Oh, Ganga! Let Rama, the son of the emperor Dasaratha honour his father's command under your protection! Having dwelled in the forest in full fourteen years, may he return once more to your bank with his brother, Lakshmana and myself! Oh, blessed

goddess Ganga! Returning safely, with all my desires fulfilled, I shall worship you with great joy.

You, Oh goddess flowing through three regions (namely heaven, earth and subterranean regions), include in your basin the realm of Brahma (the outermost of the six spheres enveloping the earth) and are vividly seen on this terrestrial plane as a consort of the ocean king. Oh, charming goddess! I, Seetha, greet you and extol you too. When Rama the tiger among men safely returns and regains his kingdom, I shall give away a lakh of cows, soft clothing and food to brahmanas with intent to please you. After reaching back the city of Ayodhya, I shall worship you with thousand pots of spirituous liquor and jellied meat with cooked rice well prepared for the solemn rite. (Ramayana [2.52.89])[27]

Varuni finds mention in the Valmiki Ramayana as well, which describes the highways of Kishkindha, the capital city of the monkey brothers Vali and Sugriva, as being redolent with the smell of alcohol. When Rama installs Sugriva as the king of Kishkindha, he is promised help by the huge army of monkeys in finding Sita. Many months pass and Rama, angry at Sugriva for reneging on his promise, sends Lakshmana to remind him of his vow to help. Lakshmana, too, gets upset as he is made to wait outside Sugriva's bedroom. Angered, Lakshmana shouts that he will break down the door, when it is opened by a dishevelled, inebriated and half-naked Tara, Vali's widow. In an attempt to calm Lakshmana, Tara asks if he knows the story of Sage Vishwamitra, who forgot everything else the moment he set eyes on the celestial *apsara* Menaka. 'If that was the case with sages, what could one expect of a mere monkey?' she asks, indicating that Sugriva was too intoxicated and in no condition to meet him.

---

While Lord Rama is a man who abides completely by dharma – nothing that he is depicted as doing can ever be construed as being unrighteous – Krishna, on the other hand, is all things to all people: He is friend and philosopher, student and guru, cowherd and king, lover and god. He is also the epitome of humans with all their failings and foibles, loves and hatreds. So, it's hardly surprising that Krishna is depicted as dancing with the gopis or drinking with his friends. Whether real or fictional, the great love of Krishna's life is Radha, with whom he spent a great deal of time while in

Brindavan. He also resides in the hearts of every gopi with whom he performs the *raas lila*.

> Then the two [Krishna and Radha], O brahmana, being tired due to many pastimes proper for the time in the groves, resort, with their attendants, to the foot of a tree, and sitting there drank liquor, O best sage. There the two, intoxicated due to the liquor, with their eyes closed due to sleep, held each other's hands, being under the influence of Cupid's arrows. All their friends too, intoxicated by wine, and with their eyes troubled by sleep sat around in the charming bowers. (Padma Purana [5.83.53–59a])[28]

In the Udyoga Parva of the Mahabharata, Sanjaya, the charioteer of King Dhritarashtra, is sent to deliver a message to Krishna who is staying with the Pandavas and reports back to the king:

> Sanjaya said, 'Listen, O king, as I tell thee the state in which I found Krishna and Dhananjaya ... With looks bent down and hands joined together, and with senses well restrained, I entered the inner apartments for conferring with those gods among men. Neither Abhimanyu nor the Twins can repair to that place

> where are the two Krishnas and Draupadi and lady Satyabhama. There I beheld those chastisers of foes, exhilarated with *Bassia* wine, their bodies adorned with garlands of flowers … And I beheld Kesava's feet resting upon Arjuna's lap while those of the high-souled Arjuna rested upon the laps of Krishna and Satyabhama.' (Mahabharata [5.59])[29]

Krishna was not the only one in the Mahabharata who drank alcohol; the Pandavas did too, as did the sons of Krishna, both Samba and Pradyumna. Once, the venerable sage Narada came to Dwarka to meet Lord Krishna and was respectfully greeted by all the young Yadavas there, beginning with Pradyumna, Krishna's eldest son. But Samba (Krishna's son through his wife Jambavati) chose to ignore Narada. Proud of his youth, good looks, virility and deluded by his own grandeur, Samba was constantly indulging in sexual dalliances and liquor. Angered at being ignored by Samba, Narada decided to teach him a lesson.[30]

---

By the time the Grihya Sutras were written, around 500 BCE, alcohol had become so prevalent that it found its way into these works of domestic rituals and rites meant for householders. In a culture that did and still does consider that guests should be treated as gods – *Atithi devo bhava* – to offer food and drink to guests was considered to be the greatest gift that one could give others. Food, for which people toiled long and hard, and drink were not to be denigrated but to be taken very seriously.

So, not surprisingly, a rather long list of different types of alcohol makes its appearance in the sutras. What had started out initially as sacred and exclusive oblations to gods found its way into society, becoming a regular feature in coronations, weddings, ceremonies and, most importantly, festivals. Drinking of alcohol is routinely mentioned in festival literature and believed to greatly add to the merriment of the occasion. Songs and dancing, music and liquor are all variously described in the Ratnavali, written by the great dramatist Harsha, as a typical and necessary aspect of many festivals – like Holi, which used to be known as Madanotsav, the festival of Madana or Kamadeva, the god of love.

Kama's affiliation with intoxication and passion too is well known in Hindu mythology. In the Sanatkumara Samhita, he is accompanied by his friends Varuni (wine),

Raga (love, affection, amorous or sexual sentiment) and Mada (intoxication). So, it is not surprising that both he and Sura were traditionally evoked at all fertility rites, especially at wedding ceremonies. The procreative potentialities of marriage were called to the fore by sprinkling the bride with wine and evoking Kama, symbolically generating passion.

> Kama you are intoxication by name. Bring him (the bridegroom) so that he may be here together with the bride. To thee there is Sura, here may there be excellent birth. Hail![31]

> Whatever lustre there is in dice, whatever lustre is in wine, whatever lustre is in cows, Asvins, endow this dame therewith. With all the sheen that balmeth wine, or thigh of female paramour. With all the sheen that balmeth dice, even with this adorn the dame. (Atharva Veda [14.1.35–6])[32]

---

According to the eminent historian Dr Moti Chandra's work titled *Kashi ka Ithihaas* (the history of Kashi), vestiges of the festival known as 'the Madirotsava can still be seen in the present-day Piyala ka Mela, a fair held in Varanasi sometime in Nov–Dec at the Chauka Ghats and at Shivpur. At this fair, before the festivities begin, the first toasts are offered to Kalika Brahmani and Satya Chamarin – two women from either end of the caste scale who loved their liquor.' According to the book, royal families too went on picnics on Madhupanotsava (drinking festival) day with the ladies of the court, where they sang, danced and abandoned themselves to the influence of alcohol.[33]

—

Settled agriculture resulted in surplus food production and stability, which in turn led to a burgeoning population, leading to stratification and divisions within society. Ancient thinkers presented the varna or caste system as being of divine origin and as the natural order of society and classified into groups of Brahmins, Kshatriyas, Vaishyas and Shudras.

With the classification of society into the four varnas, everything – education, vocations, relationships, community festivities – got stratified, including the consumption of alcohol. The most affected, ironically, were the very priests who had so revelled in the outstanding qualities of Soma but were now prohibited from drinking Sura. The justification was that priests were seen as upholders of dharma and the ones who taught scriptures to others, and could therefore not be seen in a state of intoxication; the only exception was that Sura could be consumed by priests while conducting certain yagnas, like the Sautramani Yagna.

Ancient India, so very fond of its classifications, also devised a hierarchy for who could drink and how much, and what kind of drinks were permissible. On top of the list were the Brahmins who were permitted around 10 measures, the Kshatriyas eight and the Shudras six. Kshatriyas and Vaishyas were permitted to drink only certain varieties of alcohol like madhu (wine distilled from grapes) and sidhu (distilled from molasses). Consuming this was not considered to be a transgression as 'they drank only the liquors that were permitted to be consumed by Kshatriyas, and not the forbidden variety'.[34]

Women, too, were permitted to drink, with the exception of Brahmin ladies who could drink only kaira, a drink made from coconuts, honey and molasses. Widows, virgins and menstruating women, however, had to totally abstain. According to the Manusmriti, women who drank in the company of men other than their husbands were derided and were known as *unmadini* – mad women – whereas women who drank in the company of their husbands were permitted only a fourth of what their husbands consumed.

Punishments for transgressions were also codified:

> A twice-born person, having drunk wine though folly, Should drink red-hot wine, he then becomes free from guilt, when his body has been completely burnt by it. (Manusmriti [11.8.90])[35]

There were several expiations for transgressions, especially for Brahmins. If a Brahmin got drunk, he had to perform what was known as the Krcchracandrayana expiation or he could repeat the Gayatri Mantra or Jatavedasa Mantra ten thousand times, which made him pure again.

The purification process for Kshatriyas was half of what the Brahmins were expected to do. But usually, atonements were nothing more than a dip in the Ganges or, in extreme cases, the donation of a cow or two.

Soon, instruction manuals such as the Katyayana Srauta Sutra sprang up that explained in vivid detail the preparation, germination and filtration processes involved in the making of Sura, which could easily be distilled by everyone. According to contradictory and confusing laws, alcohol distilled from grains was to be called Sura, but this was expressly prohibited for the three higher castes, says the Manusmriti:

> Wine indeed is the dirty refuse of grains, and sin also is called 'dirt'; for this reason the Brahmaṇa, the Kshatriya and the Vaishya shall not drink wine. (Manusmriti [11.8.93])[36]

Other distils from grains, coconut and palm trees and fruits were free for all.

---

By the end of the Vedic era, the use of alcohol was widespread, having shed all pretensions of being 'holy' or 'spiritual'. The priests, who were initially the primary consumers of Soma and Sura, began to resent its usage by the general public and went from being advocates to vociferous and vehement opponents.

As so often happens, whenever religion transforms into dogma and a rigid set of beliefs, practices and rituals, backlash is inevitable. Soon, individuals and entire communities boxed in by Brahminical traditions cast themselves as being beyond the pale of orthodoxy. The power and relevance of these Vedic priests began to decline, giving rise to religious changes, new movements and the first pan-Indian empire.

—

The Mauryan Empire, established in 322 BCE by Chandragupta Maurya, marked a milestone in the history of Ancient India. Going beyond geographical territories, it became the first empire to rule over much of the Indian subcontinent, giving it a strong, centrally controlled administration. Under the Mauryas, trade and commerce flourished, as did agriculture and the arts.

The Arthashastra is a treatise on politics, economics, military strategy, governance and social organization attributed to the philosopher and prime minister of the empire Kautilya, also known as Chanakya, who was instrumental in establishing the reign of Chandragupta Maurya. While primarily a handbook on statecraft and an instruction manual for Chandragupta, it is not just restricted to politics, military strategy, economics or marriage but also explores the pursuit of worldly goods and desires, personal success, stability and social status.

And since it was a manual for the king, it naturally also brings up the issue of alcohol. The first known mention of honey-based wines in the Indian subcontinent comes from the Arthashastra, where Chanakya, although critical of the emperor's and his courtiers' widespread use of alcohol, pens down a special honey-based wine called madhu.

Liquor had, until then, been ritualistic and communal; there was no mention of revenue or taxes. Under the Mauryas, it became a very big source of revenue to the exchequer but remained under careful scrutiny because Kautilya realized that excessive intake of liquor would be a societal problem. A keen observer of human behaviour, he understood that men would after all be men and that prostitution, gambling and drinking had become an intrinsic part of social life. So, rather than clamping down and imposing prohibition, he laid down norms and laws for moderating and monitoring all these activities. For instance, prostitutes had to have regular health checks and had recourse to law if they were not paid or ill-treated; gambling too had its rules for settling debts and the manufacture and use of alcohol was closely monitored. The Arthashastra highlights three aspects of brewing: the economy of the grain, brewing technologies and laws to control consumption, that is, the management of drunkenness.

---

Modern-day India has inherited a lot from Chandragupta Maurya. It was during his reign that the sale of liquor first came to be controlled and taxed. Realizing how widespread the use of alcohol was and that the liquor business was lucrative, he made its production a monopoly of the state, with the exception of physicians, who were permitted to brew alcohol for medicinal purposes. Special jobs with titles such as 'superintendents of liquor' were created for people who were familiar with the production and distribution of alcohol and other fermented brews. Their job was to control and regulate the traffic of liquor into forts, towns and the countryside. Depending on demand and supply, they also had the power to centralize or decentralize the sale of liquor. A fine of 600 panas would be imposed on all offenders other than those who were manufacturers, purchasers or sellers of liquor. There were also rules on where the liquor shops were to be located (not too close to one another) and liquor could not be taken out of villages and sold outside.

There was an interesting caveat though: Liquor could be taken out of the tavern only by persons of 'pure, good character', and even then, only in limited quantities. Everyone else whose character was not quite up to scratch was restricted to drinking inside the tavern. If any of these people were found in possession of articles that did not belong to them, especially gold or silver, they were immediately arrested. Even those who had money were not permitted extravagances or binge drinking; they too were arrested. In another departure, although Soma was allowed for religious ceremonies, it was excluded from domestic rituals and substitutes were listed instead.

Prices, too, were controlled by the government. No fresh liquor, other than bad liquor, could be sold below a minimum price. Liquor that had turned bad was either sold or given to slaves or workmen in lieu of wages, or fed to beasts of burden or hogs.

There appears to have been a lively pub culture, with every village having at least one tavern. These *madhushala*s, as the bars came to be called, were not just meant for drinking; they also contained rooms with beds to provide rest and recreation. These taverns were regularly inspected and expected to be kept neat and clean, with comfortable seats and linen and plenty of water, and decorated with flowers. Spies were stationed outside liquor shops to ensure that people did not drink away their incomes. There was also policing inside the bars to ensure that inebriated wealthy patrons were not robbed of their money and jewels, and if any theft occurred, the bar owner became liable and had to make good the loss. The bars were also good places to keep an eye on foreigners in case they were spies.

Public street drinking was permitted only during festivals and for no more than four days; anybody found flouting rules was fined. On festivals, fair days and pilgrimages, the state issued a licence to manufacture liquor, and the superintendent would go around collecting fees from those who were issued these liquor licences. Women and children were allowed to collect Sura and kinva, which was the name for the fermenting agent, free of cost.

The Mauryan Empire was so large that it also imported wines and liquors from neighbouring regions. Those who traded in liquor, with the exception of the king, had to pay a 5 per cent toll to bring it into Pataliputra, the capital city. At the end of the day, the superintendent had to calculate the total sales under the various heads of different kinds of liquor, and from the moneys realized, a fixed amount would be deposited into the exchequer. Foreign liquor merchants and those who imported liquor had to pay a higher percentage.

Alcohol occupies a whole chapter in the Arthashastra, and so it comes as no surprise that since the prices and levies varied according to the brews, there are numerous varieties with specific names and percentages of alcohol mentioned in the text. There were asavas and *arishtas*; *kapasayani*, the name given to white wine; *harahuraka*, red wine that was transported from a place near present-day Kabul; *maireya*, a spiced sugar-based drink exclusively drunk by royalty; and *varuni*, which had a high alcohol percentage, besides several others. All attest to its importance as a source of revenue as well as its significance in society.

---

The influence of the empire, and the Arthashastra in particular, did not wane with the decline of the Mauryas; the influence persisted well into the common era when, as large kingdoms flourished and societies grew exponentially, it became imperative to bring in the rule of law and codify dharmic rules.

Probably the best-known work of these Dharma Shastras is the Manava Dharma Shastra, better known as the Manusmriti. The Code of Manu is a compilation of laws reflecting Hindu thought preserved in 2,685 verses. It is one of the first legal texts and is an abridged and rewritten version of a much older text that purports to have been a discourse between Manu, the mind-born son of Brahma, and the erudite sage Bhrigu. It became the foundation of Hindu Law – a systemic code of the then prevalent laws, customs and traditions. While the exact date of the Manusmriti is unknown, it's generally accepted to have been written in early Sanskrit, sometime between the third and second centuries BCE. The text explores the concepts of dharma, caste structures, the definitions of virtue and morality, laws for proper conduct, relationships, the duties of householders and, of course, the use and abuse of alcohol – tenets that got modified with every rewrite. The Manusmriti lays special emphasis on the three 'upper castes', which is oftentimes contradictory.

The consumption of alcohol is addressed with varying levels of restriction based on caste. While the Kshatriyas are allowed to consume alcohol in moderation as part of their social and ceremonial functions, the Brahmins have to abstain due to their spiritual and religious responsibilities. For the Vaishyas, too, the Manusmriti lays down specific rules and restrictions regarding alcohol consumption, conceding that the consumption of alcohol is natural and not forbidden, though adding a caveat that abstention brings great rewards.

> The ten intoxicating drinks are unclean for a Brahmana; but a Kshatriya and a Vaishya commit no wrong in drinking them. (Vishnu Smriti [22.84])[37]

And, of course, what the lower castes did or drank was no one's concern.

With the passing of time and presumably after some careful observation and deep contemplation, the wise Manu turned his attention to rooting out what he came to believe was downright evil. He laid down strict rules for the prevention of drinking, maintaining that alcohol consumption was the most pernicious of the king's vices, and constantly counselled kings to banish liquor sellers, going to the extent of advising that the drinker be branded on the forehead with the sign of the tavern (that is, the wine-cup).

Manu's rules already expounded in the Rg Veda were particularly stringent for Brahmins, who were already reeling under prohibitory orders. If caught imbibing, they were to be 'excluded from all fellowship at meals, all sacrifices, instruction, matrimonial alliances, and all religious duties'. They were to be cast off by 'paternal and maternal relations, and receive neither compassion nor salvation'.[38]

> When the 'Brahman' resident in his body has been once deluged by wine, the 'Brahmanahood' disappears and the man becomes a Sudra. (Manusmriti [11.8.97])[39]

Manu was equally hard on women who had taken up drinking.

> Drinking, associating with wicked people, separation from her husband, rambling, sleeping and residence at other's house are the six corrupters of women. (Manusmriti [9.1.13])[40]

Further, Manu stated that 'it was an offense to share her couch ... no libations were to be performed at her death; and in her next birth, she would descend into the body of a jackal or some equally low animal or would be born in hell.'[41]

Manu even went to the extent of rewriting the laws for whatever little Soma was used. While his predecessors had not just permitted but encouraged the use of liquor for religious purposes, he opposed this indulgence and was determined to put an end to it. He, therefore, put restrictions on the way Soma was manufactured and sold, branding the seller as a low-born person. He set conditions for its consumption ensuring mainly that those who drank were financially sound. The mandate in the Manusmriti was that a twice-born man should only consume Soma or perform the Soma sacrifice if he possessed enough wealth to support his depends for at least three years.

Those on the fringes of society and/or those who didn't come under the purview of the Dharma Shastras, like royalty, the aristocracy, princesses, queens and women from non-Brahminical castes like devadasis, could and did regularly enjoy their drinks without fear or inhibition.

And so it came to pass that in a span of a little over a thousand years, Soma, which had enjoyed such an exalted status, sanctioned by the gods and endorsed by sages, slowly became a distant memory to be replaced by the more proletarian Sura and other local brews. Alcohol, however, had obviously become an integral part of the cultural fabric of India, and the Mauryan kings, understanding human behaviour, wisely started regulating its sale and use rather than prohibiting it.

The spirits were here to stay.

# 2

# Nirvana and Wellness: The Middle Path

As the Vedic era transitioned into an early historic age, the widening chasms between the castes and social disparities gave rise to the Shramana Movement, the followers of which were an ascetic creed that eschewed the pomp and grandeur of Vedic Brahmanism and set out on a quest for a personal God.

By the sixth century BCE, northern India was going through big social and spiritual changes. Jainism, traced to Mahavira, directly addressed what were then seen as excesses and injustices in Vedic religion.

Around the same time was born Siddhartha Gautamam who, deeply troubled by human suffering, also sought a path beyond rituals and rigid caste hierarchies. Buddhism rose as a reformist response to the religious mores of the time, shifting focus away from expensive rituals and towards personal discipline, compassion and inner transformation.

By the seventh century BCE, even as Vedic thought evolved to reach new philosophical heights, its ritualistic excesses and the high-handedness of the Brahmin priests who conducted the prescribed rituals and rites started to rankle the common people. As the search for God and the largess that He was supposed to mete out remained elusive, increasingly joyless and a burden, more and more people cast themselves out of the pale of Vedic orthodoxy. Soon, the power and relevance of these priests began to decline due to their obsessive attachment to power, their greed and the rituals that had become unintelligible and meaningless to the common man. This was made worse as these religious formalities began to be valued more than devotion, honesty, compassion, faith and humaneness.

The rigid caste structures did not help either – a system that had gained expediency with the rising power of Brahmin priests who saw themselves as upholders of knowledge and character, and the only ones worthy of being the intermediaries between men and God. Ironically, the liberties to explore the divine and the independence of thought that had been encouraged by the ancient rishis became the foundations of protest against what had become Vedic dogma, giving rise to new religious movements.

---

The end of the Vedic period saw the rise of the Shramana traditions that rejected the authority of the priests and the Vedic centrality of rituals, which had reached epic proportions of ostentation. In direct contrast with Brahmanism and the dissolute lives led by the priests, the Shramanas – the word means to toil, labour or exert – renounced all luxuries, choosing to lead a simple life. The religions that arose from this great religious ferment were seriously ascetic in nature, renouncing caste and gender hierarchies, and even marriage and domesticity, opting for a life of severe self-discipline and abstinence in an attempt to achieve spiritual liberation.

This upheaval spawned several new philosophies like Jainism, Buddhism and the Ajivika, Carvaka and Ajnana schools.

Even though initially dismissed as being unorthodox, non-conformist and sacrilegious, these religions had their genesis in Vedic philosophy and embraced its key concepts, namely, dharma (righteousness), *samsara* (the cycle of birth and death) and *moksha* (liberation). To this mix, they added their own concepts of ahimsa, vegetarianism and simplicity of dress and living.

The first of these philosophies to be formalized into a religion was Jainism.

—

Jains claim to have existed long before the Aryans, going back to the Indus Valley Civilization. Jainism has obscure beginnings and traces its lineage to King Rishabhanatha as the first among the 24 Tirthankaras. Of these 24, the last two, Parshvanath and Mahavira (599–527 BCE) are considered to be historical figures.

Mahavira was more a reformer and propagator of an existing religious order than the founder of a new faith, reorganizing the philosophical tenets of Jainism to correspond to changing times and social circumstances. Born as Vardhamana into a royal Kshatriya family to Queen Trishala of the Licchavi clan and King Siddhartha of the Ikshvaku dynasty, he came from the same lineage as the founder Rishbhanath.

When he turned 30, Mahavira abandoned his

comfortable life, home and family to live as an ascetic in the pursuit of spiritual awakening. Shedding all worldly attachments including his clothes, he undertook severe fasts and bodily mortification in his spiritual quest, which lasted for 12 years. At the end of it, he realized perfect perception, knowledge, power and bliss, which is called *keval jnana* (pure knowledge). He spent the next 30 years travelling all over India, attracting people from all walks of life – rich and poor, kings and commoners, men and women, princes and priests, the high caste as well as untouchables.

His ideology centred around finding God though contemplation and meditation and not through the rites and rituals that had become the norm under Vedic priests. The Jains were the first major critics and opponents of Brahmanism and became a well-established sect long before Buddhism.

It was, however, not a protest movement and did differ from the Vedic tenets of the time. Believing that a living body was not merely an amalgam of flesh and blood but the abode of the soul which had the potential to achieve perfect perception, the body needed to be treated with respect and looked after, never to be abused with incorrect behaviour, wrong foods or alcohol. One of the basic tenets of Jainism, ahimsa was extended to not just human beings but to all animals, plants, micro-organisms and all beings having life or life potential.

So, for Jains, eating non-vegetarian food went against this belief, as did drinking, which because of its mind-altering potential was seen as violence or *himsa* towards oneself. There were no allowances for occasional or social drinking – Jains did not and do not consume alcohol or any fermented drinks to avoid killing the large number of microorganisms associated with the fermenting process.

Mahavira did not set out to start a new religious movement, rather he was on a personal quest for self-realization. While Jainism did find followers, they lacked missionary zeal since that was not their mandate; nor did they find royal patronage a prerequisite for the spread of any ideology. Moreover, people had until then been raised on a daily diet of Vedic myths, narratives that celebrated the excesses of gods like Indra who revelled in their sexual prowess and ability to consume huge quantities of alcohol. These indulgences, though not encouraged, were condoned, taken in stride as typical human excesses. In contrast lay the severity of Jainism, which stood for penance, meditation, fasting, restraint and detachment, concepts that were too extreme for common folk to practise.

For a more compassionate understanding of their needs, they had to wait for the Buddha.

---

Buddhism, too, emerged as part of the Shramana movement; again, not as a protest but more a reform movement within the educated classes. Though it stood firmly against the excesses of the priests as well as elaborate rituals and caste and gender discrimination, the Buddhist movement, some scholars believe, was supported mostly by Brahmins from within the system rather than being a rival movement from the outside. In its initial days, the largest number of monastics were Brahmins and Kshatriyas. From these simple beginnings, Buddhism stands today as the fourth-largest religion with over 7 per cent of the global population professing to be Buddhists. Eschewing all Vedic mythologies, gods and goddesses, being neither monotheistic or polytheistic, Buddhism follows the teachings, beliefs and spiritual practices based on those of the Buddha.

According to the *Tripitaka,* which is said to be the earliest existing record of the Buddha's life and discourses, he was born as Prince Siddhartha, son of the king of present-day Nepal. It was predicted that the prince would either become a great monarch or a Buddha – a supremely enlightened teacher, but with a rider; the attendant Brahmins told his father, King Suddhodana, that Siddhartha would rule the world only if he was kept isolated from the outside world. So, the king took great pains to ensure that his son was kept far away from the realities of life, lest it influence him to don saffron.

Surrounded by luxury and raised with great care, Siddhartha grew up and eventually got married and fathered a son. When he turned 29, tired of his cloistered existence, he set out to see more of the world; venturing out, he encountered life in all its vicissitudes, seeing poverty, death, disease, ageing and misery for the first time. Deeply troubled by this reality, he finally came across a monk who seemed unfazed by all that was going on around him. Impressed with the man's equanimity, he decided to discover how the monk managed to remain so serene in the midst of so much suffering.

After much introspection, Siddhartha decided that he had to leave his family and, one day, left his sleeping wife and young son to become a wandering ascetic. He travelled towards Varanasi and visited centres of learning, where he soon mastered several philosophies. Still dissatisfied, he set out to seek a personal experience for the ultimate quest of Nirvana or self-realization. Buddhist scriptures record that Siddhartha undertook many fasts, penances and austerities, following the Jain tradition. But even extreme practices yielded no results, so Siddhartha abandoned what he called 'extreme ascetic methods' and instead sat himself down beneath a peepal tree, vowing not to get up until he had attained enlightenment. Fighting off all temptations of worldly comforts and desires, Siddhartha finally attained Nirvana, becoming a Buddha.

Travelling to a deer park just outside Kashi where he gave his first sermon, he outlined the four guiding principles of Buddhism – that there is suffering in life, the underlying cause of suffering is desire, ending desire can end suffering and the way to end desire is following a controlled and moderate lifestyle. For the rest of his life, the Buddha taught and gathered disciples to his *sangha* or community of monks. He died at age 80, telling his monks to continue working for their spiritual liberation by following his teachings, which eventually spread from India to Central and Southeast Asia, China, Korea, Japan and, in the twentieth century, to the West.

Abandoning the extreme asceticism that Jainism had adopted, the Buddha saw excessive austerity, self-mortification and fasting, amongst other things, as unnecessary to attain enlightenment, choosing instead a more moderate ascetic lifestyle. Besides, Buddhism also developed a code for ordinary people who had families and jobs but wanted to follow Buddhism and not necessarily become ascetics. The Buddha also incorporated some of the old tenets from Hinduism in his teachings, such as how good karma could be earned by helping people, giving alms to the renunciants and providing food and clothing to the poor, all of which encouraged social support for Buddhism.

The Middle Way thus became the right path to be followed, eschewing extremism of any kind, be it asceticism or hedonism, fasting or feasting, sexual indulgence or abstinence. The Buddha taught one to train the mind through meditative practices, self-restraint and, most importantly, mindfulness in every action of life.

Alcohol and opium had existed long before the Buddha. Acutely aware of the social excesses of the time, the Buddha emphasized ethical living and laid down basic codes of conduct, which were to abstain from killing (ahimsa), stealing, lying, sexual misconduct and intoxication. Intoxication included anything that was ingested that distorted consciousness and disrupted self-awareness. The Buddha understood the subtle and pernicious nature of alcohol and included the downside of intoxication. Drinking can lead to loss of wealth, increased quarrelling, susceptibility of illness, disrepute and weakening wisdom. In a sutra in the Fifth Precept he says: 'One is to refrain from drinking even a drop of alcohol and taking intoxicants because they are the cause of heedlessness. If any Buddhist succumbs to the lure of intoxicating drinks, they shall not consider me as a teacher.'[1]

Strict strictures however did nothing to deter a population used to drinking. Despite warnings from the Buddha, people continued to consume alcohol. Understanding that imposing extreme restrictions of any kind would not go down well with the people and would deter them from accepting Buddhism, the Buddha, although prohibiting alcohol, advocated moderation in everything. Though not considered to be a sin, it was not the alcohol itself that was dangerous but what it did to one's mind, mindfulness being a very basic tenet of Buddhism.

What Buddhists abhor is not alcohol but intoxication, which can be interpreted to mean drinking more than the body can handle. There are records of prominent Buddhists who drank reasonable quantities of alcohol without getting intoxicated. Alcohol and drugs were seen as an escape route from reality, so the most important reason for prohibition was the effect of alcohol on the mind and to stay in the present. According to the Buddha's teachings, drinking affects Samyaktva (Right Faith and Right Knowledge) and is a deterrent to spiritual progress. Alcohol would thus impair decision-making, degrade judgement, loosen inhibitions and lead people to speak and act in ways that were harmful to themselves and others.

This is a popular, oft-repeated Buddhist story. Once, a Buddhist monk came across a woman who set out to seduce him. She threatened to commit suicide if the monk did not do one of three things: have sex with her, kill a goat for a party or drink the alcohol she had brought for him. The monk thought long and hard and considered his options. Losing his celibacy and killing animals was a cardinal sin as taught by the Buddha. On the other hand, not taking any action would result in the death of the woman. So, deciding that drinking was the lesser sin, he started on the alcohol. Sure enough, he got inebriated and, getting hungry, killed the goat and consumed it, after which he also had sex with the woman. This was a parable used often by the Buddha to teach the effects of drinking and to demonstrate that alcohol seriously affects rational thinking.

Despite this, there was considerable ambivalence regarding the use of alcohol. In a throwback to early Vedic practices, there are references in Buddhist scriptures that indicate that, like the Brahmins, Tantric and Tibetan Buddhist monks too offered alcohol to deities as one of the five precious elements (*dutsi*). They believed that alcohol was actually a precious divine element with nurturing and healing qualities; it was its abuse that caused problems, with the abuser to be blamed and not the alcohol. It was also considered to have medicinal values if used judiciously. Enlightened monks and saints drank small amounts of alcohol for their health while believing that only ordinary people drank in excess. In one interesting debate on the merits and demerits of alcohol, one side hailed it as a drink of gods, kings and courtiers, rich and ordinary people, an elixir that was both a relaxant and energizer, while the other side held alcohol to be responsible for confusing the senses, leading to negative deeds, unacceptable behaviour and health problems. The debate ends with a word of caution to use alcohol judiciously.

A fair warning that has not been taken seriously over three millennia.

Buddhism found easy acceptance as the Buddha preached not in Sanskrit but in Pali and Prakrit, languages easily understood by all classes of people. More importantly, he used metaphors and taught through narratives and parables that men and women, young and old could easily identify with. The Jataka Tales form a voluminous body of sacred Buddhist literature, a compendium of some 550 anecdotes and fables that follow the incarnations and births, both in animal and human forms, of Siddhartha Gautama before he becomes the Buddha. The Jataka Tales are dated between 300 and 400 CE and are essentially tales with a moral. They have a vast canvas of characters who get into all sorts of trouble and dilemmas, whereupon the Buddha intervenes and resolves the issues. These then became part of the essential teachings of the Buddha. Of these there are 35 tales that were collected for the purposes of teaching and make up the *Cariya Pitaka* or 'Basket of Conduct'.

The Jataka Tales reflect the societal norms and issues of the period. A large number of the Jatakas originally belonged to earlier Indian folklore; including these and using them as the basis for his teachings enabled the

Buddha to reach larger audiences. Combined with his philosophy, these Jataka Tales, down-to-earth folklore, taught values and virtues that inspired and became exemplars for all of humanity. In one such Jataka Tale, there is a reference to Madirotsava, a Bacchanalian festival in which the king of Kashi distributes alcohol to all his subjects. During one such orgy, the tale says, even holy men got drunk and went around creating mayhem, shouting and having fist-fights before they finally dropped into a stupor.

Much like the Vedic mythologies that created narratives for the genesis of Soma and Sura, the Buddhists, too, have a story of genesis that closely mimics Balarama's discovery of Sura.

Once, while staying in Jeta Vana, one of the best-known Buddhist viharas, the Master narrated a tale about 500 women who were friends of Vishaka, a wealthy aristocratic woman who was considered to be the chief female patron of the Buddha. These women were all drinkers of strong liquor. Once, during a Madirotsava, these 500 women, after providing alcohol to their masters, decided that they too would participate in the festival. They went to Vishaka and said, 'Friend, we also want to celebrate the feast.' She replied that it was a festival of drinking, and she did not consume alcohol. They said, 'You then make an offering to the Buddha, but we will celebrate.' She readily gave her consent.

As evening set in, they all set off for Jeta Vana to listen to the Buddha. The women had by then had too much to drink but nonetheless accompanied Vishaka to see the Master. Even as Vishaka paid her obeisance to the Master, the already-inebriated women started singing and dancing seductively. Others started quarrelling and shouting at each other and chaos reigned. Seeing this the Master emitted a strong ray of light from his eyebrow, followed by blinding darkness. Terrified and frightened by the possibility of death, the women immediately became sober as the effect of alcohol wore off. The Master then advised the women to give up their wanton ways and follow the path of the Buddha.

On witnessing the mayhem caused by her drunken friends, Visakha asked the Master, 'Holy sir, whence has arisen this alcohol that violates a man's honour and conscience?'

The Master then tells Visakha the following tale:

Once, when King Brahmadatta ruled Kashi, a forester went to the Himalayas to gather herbs and wood. There he came across a tall tree with a big hole in the centre that often got filled with water when it rained. Around it grew fruit trees and a pepper vine, the ripe fruits from which fell into the hole. Parrots sitting on the tree would pluck the heads of grain and some sheaves of paddy would also fall into this hole. With the intense heat of the sun, the fruit and paddy turned into a fermented drink which was consumed by flocks of birds. Intoxicated by the toddy they'd drunk, they would fall off to sleep until the effect wore off and then flew away rather happily. This happened to all the animals like squirrels and monkeys that drank this water.

Curious and intrigued by what he'd witnessed, the forester adventurously tried it himself and, sure enough, promptly fell into an intoxicated stupor. On waking, hungry, he killed the partridges perched on the tree, roasted them and spent the next two days drinking and eating happily. Not far from the tree lived an ascetic named Varuna, whom the forester was acquainted with. He then decided that he'd like to share his new-found elixir with the sage and, filling a reed pipe, he offered the liquor along with some roast meat to the holy man.

The story however does not end there. Believing that they were on to a good thing, they filled many reed pipes with alcohol; reaching the village, they sent a message to the king that they were wine merchants who had come with an exclusive offer. Intrigued, the king sent for them, tasted some of the liquor and got intoxicated. However, annoyed that it only lasted a few hours, he ordered the men to get more supplies.

The forester and holy man stayed a few days by the tree, researched the ingredients that went into making the liquor and started manufacturing it in large quantities, supplying it to all the townsmen who soon became indolent wretches. They then approached the king who invested in their wine-making business. After that, they went from city to city, leaving disastrous consequences in their wake. Finally, they arrived at Savatthi, ruled by a king called Sabbamitta, who too agreed to set up the duo in business. They set about storing the liquor in five hundred jars and, to guard them, bound a cat to each jar. Unfortunately, when the liquor fermented and started spilling over, the cats drank the strong liquor and lay down to sleep, oblivious to the world around them. Seeing this, officers informed the king that the cats had died from drinking the liquor. Angered, he ordered the two merchants to be beheaded.

However, the cats soon woke up; seeing this, the king concluded that this must be the mead that the men had promised. So, he organized an *utsav*, set up a pavilion and, surrounded by his courtiers, sat down to drink. Sakka Muni, the king of heaven, saw the king drinking and thought that the whole country would perish if this continued and that he would have to put a stop to this. So, disguised as a brahmin and holding a jar full of liquor, he approached the king, saying, 'Buy this jar, buy this jar.' King Sabbamitta, puzzled by the insolent manner of the priest, wondered who he was:

Who art thou, Being from on high,
Whose form emits bright rays of light,
Like levin flash athwart the sky,
Or moon illuming darkest night?
...Then, brahmin, who thou art declare,
And what within thy jar may be,
That thus appearing in mid-air,
Thou fain wouldst sell thy wares to me.[2]

Then Sakka Muni, expounding the evils of alcohol in over 30 verses, replies:

This jar nor oil nor ghee doth hold,
No honey or molasses here,
But vices more than can be told

…

Buy then, O king, this jar of mine,
Full to the brim of strongest wine.

Who drinks will run all shamelessly,
Like nude ascetic thro' the town,
And late take rest—so dazed is he—
Forgetting when to lay him down.

…

Buy then O king, this jar of mine,
Full to the brim of strongest wine.
Wine is a thing of boastful pride,
An ugly, naked, cowardly imp,
To strife and calumny allied,
A home to shelter thief and pimp.

…

Buy then O king, this jar of mine,
Full to the brim of strongest wine.
She too that drinks will in her pride
Her husband and his sire revile,
And, dignity of race defied,
A slave to folly will beguile.

…

Buy then O king, this jar of mine,
Full to the brim of strongest wine.
Angels infatuate with wine
Fell from eternal heaven, O king,
With all their magic power divine:
Then who would taste the accursed thing?[3]

On hearing this wise counsel, the king recognized the misery caused by alcohol and gave up drinking. He ordered all the drinking vessels to be broken and his subjects to abstain from liquor.

Going by the numerous Jataka parables that use examples of inebriation and the ill-effects of liquor, it is obvious that alcohol was very prevalent in society and there was no social stigma attached to it. So, recognizing the extent of the indulgence, instead of placing a blanket ban on liquor the Buddha introduced the need for heedfulness, which in this context meant maintaining clarity of mind to understand the boundaries between what was right and what was wrong.

The Jataka Tales illustrate this with another example.

Once upon a time, when Brahmadatta was king, the city was home to a gang of drunkards who were always on the lookout for people they could defraud to feed their drinking habit. One day, having run out of money, they hit upon a scheme to rob the richest man in Kashi little realizing that he was a Bodhisattva himself.

They decided to drug a flask of alcohol, entice the man to drink it and rob him when he was in a stupor. To this end, they set up a temporary roadside bar and mixed the remaining liquor into a bottle with some strong sedatives. Soon, the wealthy man came by on his way to the palace. One of the drunks called out to him, 'Honourable Sir, why not start your day right by having a drink with us? And the first one is on the house!' He then poured a glass of the doctored liquor.

The Bodhisattva did not drink any form of alcohol but nonetheless wondered why these drunkards were so generously giving away their liquor. Realizing their chicanery, he decided to teach them a lesson. He replied, 'It would be an insult to appear before the king in a drunken state, but since you have been so kind, could you wait for me until I return from the palace?' The drunkards were disappointed but decided to be patient and wait.

Later that day, the rich man returned to the roadside bar. The alcoholics, by then desperate for a drink, pleaded with him, 'Honourable Sir, please take a drink of this fine liquor. Remember, the first one is free!' But the merchant just kept looking at the bottle of liquor and said, 'I see that the bottle and glass are exactly as they were this morning. If it were as good as you say it is, you would have drunk most of it yourselves. Instead you have waited all day for me … I'm sure you have drugged the alcohol. I'm no fool.' He then walked away, leaving the drunkards high and dry. The moral of this parable is that sobriety helps you keep your common sense.[4]

---

Over time, Buddhism spread to new lands and metamorphosed to accommodate local cultures and traditions. Emperor Asoka, horrified by the devastation caused by war, is believed to be one of the first kings to convert to Buddhism. He is said to have sent missionaries throughout the country to spread the word of the Buddha. Chinese travellers, scholars and traders all along the Silk Route carried the word of the Buddha to distant lands, where Buddhism split into two sects. The Theravada sect dominated in South Asia, whereas Mahayana Buddhism complemented Chinese Confucianism and Taoism. The religion also morphed into Zen Buddhism in Japan and Vajrayana Buddhism in Tibet.

All or most of these forms of Buddhism advise abstinence, or at the very least 'mindful drinking'.

Practitioners of Vajrayana, also known as Tantrayana since it incorporated Tantric practices, is a sect followed in India and Tibet that incorporates alcohol as part of their practice. The intent is not to get the monks drunk but to get them to personally experience what it does to the body and thence overcome it. In neighbouring Bhutan, historical texts refer to alcohol being given as an offering during religious ceremonies as early as the seventh century, a tradition that is followed even today. According to the Bhutanese, alcohol offerings come in two forms. There is a subtle version known as *dutsi* (a sweet homemade distilled spirit), which is offered during ritualistic religious rites in a human skull cup. At the end of the ceremony, the dutsi, which is believed to have acquired divine blessings, is distributed to worshippers. The other, more socialized version, called *marchang*, is used during ceremonies to evoke deities' blessings when embarking on new ventures. Bhutanese babies are introduced to alcohol soon after they are born, when a special homemade rice-based fermented drink called *chhang khoy* is served to entertain guests as well as nourish and sedate the mother. The child, of course, receives alcohol through breast milk from the mother.[5]

Though Burmese Buddhists, for too long, held the belief that it was unacceptable for a monk to drink, they have *nat*s in their popular folk history, god-like spirits that are venerated in conjunction with Buddhism. These spirits are propitiated with liquor and meat, harking back to pre-Buddhist society in Burma. An inscription dated to 1248, found in Bagan, contains the earliest-known reference to the word 'arak', a word frequently used for alcohol in India.

---

Buddhism's central tenets forbid drunkenness and drinking in any quantity, but some sects used esoteric methods to attain Nirvana, such as Tantric Buddhism. The word 'Tantra' usually conjures images of sexual orgies because of its association with extreme practices. Tantra, however, is an ancient Indian religious movement that seeks to harness mental and physical experiences and energies for use on the path to enlightenment. Following on the heels of Indian Tantric practices, Buddhist Tantra probably first appeared between the third and sixth centuries CE, eventually spreading to many parts of Asia. Today, Buddhist Tantra is primarily found in all of the

Tibetan lineages as well as in Japanese Buddhism, especially Shingon.

Tantra tries to go beyond just seeing the nature of reality. It is about striving to achieve a state of Buddhahood and tapping into one's own potential to become Buddha. Tantric practices involve the use of elaborate rituals and visualizations, including working with sound through chanting mantras (sacred words and phrases), with gesture through mudras (ritualized sacred hand gestures), with sight through visualizations and mandalas (diagrams of the universe) and with vital energies through meditation and yoga. Mahayana Buddhism is the umbrella under which Tantric Buddhism resides and has historically been understood as being more ritualistic.

The practice of Tantra focuses on the transformation of items that are taboo or considered poisonous. Alcohol and meat were used in tantric rituals, with the understanding that nothing was impure to the Buddhas. So, offerings of alcohol and meat were metaphors for how something seemingly impure could transform into something pure; an oft-cited example is how beautiful lotuses emerge from dirty ponds. As such, there were many tantric feasts that included dancing, singing and sex while ingesting alcohol and consuming meat.

Operating at the margins of the *sangha*s and society, some of these practices adopted extreme and esoteric behaviour. The Diamond Mandala, for example, which is based on the Vajrasekhara Sutra, has naked tantriks dancing and drinking from skull cups.

The Guhyagarbha Tantra states:

> It is improper for meat and alcohol to be lacking, for these are substances enjoyed by yogis who, by means of their practices are able to overcome the power of their thoughts. Such practitioners bless the substances of the sacred feast, transforming them into amrita. And when they consume them, alcohol is no longer ordinary; neither is their attitude one of indulgence. Within this state of great purity and equality, their perceptions they experience themselves as the deity and alcohol as amrita. In such circumstances, all yogis and yoginis are allowed to consume alcohol.[6]

The value of Tantric Buddhism centres on the transformative and mind-altering quality of alcohol, which made it possible to shed one's sense of self, at least momentarily. And this, as we have seen, was not unique to Tantric Buddhism but a fact known to most religions around the world.

With the rise of Buddhism and its ascetism, the 'social meaning' of liquor and intoxication changed. Buddhist priests stayed away from alcohol, which was viewed as 'polluting', expressing their disdain for the rites and ritual use of alcohol that had been practised by Vedic priests for centuries. Despite the edicts of the Buddha, though, the rulers as well as the general population continued to eat and drink as they had in the past. His dire warnings did not deter anyone.

The Buddha might not have been able to alter the country's views on alcohol and opiates, but both Jainism and Buddhism exerted a huge influence on the Indian psyche as well as its literature, art and architecture. Both these religions gave rise to literature in Pali, and in several Sanskrit dialects such as Prakrit, used by the common people.

Ironically, the growing influence of Buddhism was most keenly experienced in South India, which, freed from stringent Brahmanical tenets, saw a resurgence of literature and music, and a revival of the carefree way of life that the southerners were used to.

—

The decline of Brahmanical ritualistic dominance coincided with the rise of new knowledge systems. Amongst these, the most influential was Ayurveda.

No book on alcohol can be complete without talking about its uses in medicine, especially in alchemy and Ayurveda, as described in works such as the Charaka Samhita, Sushruta Samhita and Madhava Nidhanam, amongst others.

The term 'Ayurveda' is composed of two Sanskrit words, *ayu*, which means 'life', and *veda*, which is translated as 'knowledge', and is deeply intertwined with India's spiritual, philosophical and cultural traditions. It is much more than a medical discourse – it is rather a system that seeks balance between the body, mind, spirit and environment.

The lockdowns brought on by the spread of Covid-19 in 2020 resulted in trauma, stress, anxieties and damage caused to countless people all around the world. Amongst the various issues that India grappled with then was the non-availability of alcohol for almost a year as the lockdowns kept getting extended indefinitely. But in times of need, Indians can be both ingenious and creative.

In a story that appeared in *ThePrint* in 2020, Manoj Kaloor, a member of the Central Council of Indian

Medicine, a now-dissolved body that oversaw higher education in Ayurveda and other Indian medical systems, told the magazine that since the lockdown, Ayurvedic pharmacies across Kerala had seen a 20 per cent increase in sales. This was because the 'arishtams and asavams' that were being sold had alcohol as their base. He also said that boards had sprung up all over town saying that these herbal concoctions were strictly for medicinal purposes. An *arishtam* is an Ayurvedic tonic or concoction prepared by fermenting medicinal herbs and contains up to 10 per cent alcohol. 'There has been a lot of publicity created through social media that arishtams can satiate alcohol urges,' Kaloor said, adding, 'non-availability of liquor in the market may be driving people to consume large quantities of these herbal drugs.'[7]

Blame it on the Sushruta and the Charaka Samhita, two ancient foundational texts that set the base for the system of medicine that is Ayurveda. The Sushruta Samhita was written in the sixth century BCE, around the time of the Buddha, by a famous physician and surgeon called Sushruta who taught at a university in Kashi. A Sanskrit text on medicine and surgery, it is one of the most important treatises to survive from the ancient world; Sushruta is known as probably the world's first plastic surgeon, as the text deals with rhinoplasty, amongst other surgeries. The Sushruta Samhita is of great historical importance as it includes unique chapters describing surgical training, instruments and operational procedures. While using alcohol as a base for some of its tinctures, it addresses an important issue of the times and dedicates an entire chapter (Chapter 27, 'Panatyaya') to alcohol, its uses and effects and the treatment of alcoholism.

This was followed by another work on medicine written around the first century CE by Agnivesha, a disciple of the Ayurvedic scholar Punarvasu Atreya. Each of his six disciples went on to compose their own samhitas that were collated and together came to be known as the Charaka Samhita, which delves into all aspects of medicine, including the logic and philosophy behind Indian medicinal systems.

Ayurveda is seen as a comprehensive system of healthcare that deals with systemic diagnosis, as well as the preventive and curative aspects of disease. It covers subjects such as foetal generation and development, human anatomy and the function and malfunction of the body. Needless to say, the use of alcohol was widespread, as both works describe the various types of wines available, the substances they are made of and the various stages of intoxication, with special emphasis on the management of drinking and control. These treatises that are almost 2,500 years old could well be a manual from Alcoholics Anonymous, albeit with Sanskrit nomenclature.

The Charaka Samhita dedicates the entirety of Chapter 24 to an in-depth discussion on alcohol, its effects and uses and treatments for alcoholism. In Ayurveda, tinctures and drinks are often made with a specific health condition in mind and are referred to as *madya*; these produce the state of intoxication known as *mada*, which, in the right proportions, brings about strength and joy, and reduces dread and stress. Recognizing the rather dire effects that Soma had on Brahmins, the book also states that Sura was prepared to provide relief for priests after performing too many yagnas and was, ironically, considered a healthier option than Soma.

These are alcoholic beverages that have medical benefits rather than being poisonous substances. In these texts, alcoholism and its withdrawal are described as *madatyaya*, which Ayurveda is capable of treating. Based on its usage, madya is categorized into two kinds, as medication and as a beverage.

The Sushruta, for example, examines the symptoms and medical treatment of alcoholism and kindred maladies (*panatyaya-pratishedha*). It describes wine as something that is acidic in nature, generates heat, dehydrates, stimulates and increases appetite. It however also has the potential to suspend all cognitive processes, entering into every limb and member of the body by reason of its subtlety (*sukshmatva*) and destroying *kapha* as well as semen.

To derive the proper use of wine, Sushruta recommends that it be drunk with a meal like cooked meat and boiled rice with ghee. Drinking on an empty stomach is dangerous, says the text, leading to rapid intoxication. Excessive drinking produces incidental nescience, which clouds the senses, destroys all self-control and publicizes the innermost thoughts of the intoxicated person.

The book also codifies three stages of intoxication.

> The first or preliminary stage … is marked by an exhilarated state of mind with increased valour and conviviality as well as a sense of well-being and talkativeness. The second or intermediate stage is indicated by incoherent speech, exhilaration and the performance of improper acts. In the third or last stage the man lies down unconscious, bereft of all powers of action, of memory and of judging the ethic effects of his acts.[8]

Labelled as dangerous, wine is also prohibited by the Sushruta Samhita in certain cases. It should not be taken by a person who is undergoing mental stress like anger, grief, fright, thirst or hunger. Its use is prohibited immediately after a long journey, after physical exercise or while eating acidic food, or if suffering from the effects of heat.

In what may seem hilarious to us today, or even tempting, what is recommended is:

> [to be surrounded by objects] which are pleasing to the five sense-organs and gratifying to the mind and heart … light wine should be always prescribed … and the patient should be enlivened with the embrace of handsome and youthful damsels … with splendid hips and thighs with their slender waists drooping under the weight of the exuberance of their breasts.[9]

If the hangover persists:

> I shall describe the cooling measures which should be employed for alleviating the burning sensation … in the case of a rich patient. The body of such a patient under the circumstances should be smeared at the outset with *Chandana* (white sandal wood)

> pastes made cooler by the contact of cold beams of the moon, pearl-necklaces and the water produced from melted ice. He should be laid down in a bed of full-blown lotus flowers sparkling with dew drops or of lotus-leaves sprinkled with spray of translucent water, and youthful damsels decked with necklaces and bangles … should be asked to touch him. He should try to alleviate the burning feeling by strolling on the banks of a tank in a garden in the soft, cool and sweet breeze bearing on its wings the soft perfume of *Kalhara* (red) lotus and water-moss dancing in the adjoining tank.[10]

The remedy for intoxication appears to be rather erotic, with another passage in the text recommending:

> Young and beautiful damsels with their full and thick-set breasts and thighs anointed with sandal pastes, being clad in wet clothes (adhering to and advantageously showing the splendid contours of their limbs, etc.,) and with their necklaces and girdles loosely sliding down their bosoms and slender waists should lie there with the man in their firm embrace. These damsels should refresh him with their secret charms in that lonely chamber and … their bodily

coolness would be able to alleviate the burning sensation of aggravated Pitta due to overdrinking.[11]

The text ends with prescriptions and remedies, recommending wines to be mixed with various herbs, dried ginger, honey, etc. that make it palatable.

These classics over and again maintain that alcohol has the ability to reach the heart and quickly, which has a direct effect on all qualities and dosas. The ultimate outcome is that our deep vitality or *ojas* will be lost, and over time, alcohol consumption will only create anxiety, agitation, disease and, finally, death.

There are as many critics of Ayurveda as there are followers. Westerners typically scoff at the esoteric philosophies, the combination of arbitrary physiological and psychological archetypes and anatomical speculations. But at the very outset, Ayurveda proclaims: Ayurveda is that which deals with the good, bad, happy and unhappy life, its promoters and non-promoters. The foundation for a healthy life, it reiterates, is not asceticism and avoidance, but enjoyment and appreciation of all the good things of life – appropriately, and in moderation.

Regarding alcohol, the Charaka Samhita is extremely sensible and pragmatic, as one can infer from the fact that a very large section (Volume 2, pages 390–408) is devoted to the correct manner of drinking alcohol as well as its management. Alcohol taken appropriately produces invigorating effects: it promotes appetite, stimulates the power of digestion, improves voice and complexion, increases strength and decreases fear fatigue and grief. It also promotes erotic passion and hilarity even in people of old age.

Proper application of these factors is called Yukti or appropriateness and then the person does not suffer from the evil effects of drinking.

The Charaka concludes with a wise warning:

> Wine is like nectar for that who drinks according to prescribed methods, in proper quantity, at proper times, with wholesome food…on the contrary it acts like poison for those who indulge in drinking unwholesome wine…observing rough regimens.[12]

So, the key lessons to be learnt about alcohol from physicians from the past 2,500 years – as indeed even now – is moderation.

# 3

# Spirited South: Southern Libertines

Most of the caste divisions, the mythologies, the Vedic rites and rituals and Sanskrit emanated from and was restricted to the North. Southern India largely enjoyed freedom from the strictures imposed by the Vedas. The rigid caste segregations and hierarchies of worship never existed.

The culture of the South during the Sangam period (500 BCE–300 CE) was thus different in spirit from that of the Vedic North. It saw literature and art flourish among common men and women – the people who tilled the fields and put their lives into verse. Life was easy, liberal and more democratic.

Alcohol here flowed freely and without inhibition, dating back to the Roman times, as the coastal regions traded and brewed toddy and arrack, a long tradition that is still alive and well today.

Much of the taught history of India is the story of North India – the Indus Valley Civilization, the advent of the Aryans, settlements along the Indo-Gangetic plain, the Mauryans, Guptas and Mughals – almost as though the lands below the Deccan Plateau were barren and uninhabited, devoid of any civilization.

On the contrary, South India did not just exist; it also flourished.

---

For over 2,000 years, the sandy beaches in present-day Puducherry have been abuzz with frenzied activity. Merchant ships from as far as Rome docked here laden with precious goods and left carrying equally exotic cargo. The port where the ships landed was called Arikamedu, located on the banks of Ariyankuppam River. Considered to be an Indo-Roman trading post from as early as the second century BCE, Arikamedu's ties with Rome began during the reign of Augustus Caesar, the first Roman emperor. These trading posts extended all along the Coromandel Coast, right up to Barigaza (Bharuch in Gujarat). Arikamedu, Comari

(Cape Comorin) and several other flourishing seaports find mention in a Greco-Roman text of the first century CE, called *Periplus of the Erythraean Sea,* a log of coastal landmarks and ports, as well as in the Greek geographer Ptolemy's *Geographia* of the second century CE.

Known for its exquisite indigenously made glass beads, lapidary, pottery and tiles, Arikamedu's glorious past would have gone unnoticed but for the efforts of an archaeologist and numismatist from France called Gabriel Jouveau-Dubreuil, who, in 1930, found an intaglio engraved with the bust of Augustus Caesar during an excavation at the site. Subsequently, the well-known British archaeologist Mortimer Wheeler continued with digs to find fragments of Roman amphorae, gold coins, lamps as well as red-glazed pottery, which he realized were pieces of well-known pottery from the Roman city of Arezzo in Tuscany. Wheeler's search yielded over 1,100 shards of Mediterranean amphorae, attesting to a regular and substantial trade of alcohol with the West. Arikamedu thus appears to have been a well-established and sophisticated European trading post, one replete with wine taverns serving imported wine from two-handled jars, which were typically from Aegean islands such as

Kos, also known for its exquisite wines. The grapes were mixed with seawater, which preserved the wine over long journeys. So high was the demand for these wines that merchants in Italy started producing fake Koan amphorae filled with Kos-style wines especially for the Indian market.[1]

Archaeologists also found imported tableware and especially designed wine decanters, suggesting that the people who lived there had rather extravagant and well-heeled habits. The regular trade indicates that the harbour town housed a mix of indigenous artisans and foreign businessmen and traders – Westerners who must have first imported the wines for their personal use. Wine made from grapes was unknown in South India, generating much interest in this new liquor that had travelled all the way from the birthplace of Bacchus, the god of wine. Rather quickly, the locals too got hooked on to this pleasant drink.

A normal-sized amphora is believed to have held the equivalent of 36 of today's bottles; considering the price of imported wines today, the value of each amphora with the added cost of shipping, is easy to imagine.[2]

Alcohol was certainly a lucrative business.

Centuries of brisk commerce and interaction with people from all over the world made the entire coastline of South India a happening place: a place of diversity and inclusion where people of varying faiths, ethnicities and classes would intermingle freely. Domingo Paes, a Portuguese traveller who visited both the Coromandel Coast as well as the Vijayanagara kingdom, wrote, 'In these cities you will find men belonging to every nation and people … countless in number, so much so that I do not wish to write it down for fear it should be thought too fabulous.'[3]

Home to many a magnificent kingdom, South India witnessed processes of social and cultural transformation that were markedly different from what transpired in the North. Cocooned from constant migrations and invasions, the empires of the South matched the best in the North. The Raya kings of Vijayanagara, the Pallavas, Pandyas, Cholas, Cheras, Hoysalas – these were all hugely prosperous sovereign states whose kings were interested in economics, governance, architecture, the arts and literature, giving rise to sophisticated societies that have left lasting legacies.

Much of this is reflected in the towering temples, stunning sculpture and architecture as well as the vast canon of Tamil literature that has come to be known as Sangam literature. 'In their antiquity and in their contemporaneity, there is not much else in any Indian literature equal to these quiet and dramatic Tamil poems ... where passion is balanced by courtesy, transparency by ironies, impersonality by vivid detail, austerity of line by richness of implication. These poems are the earliest evidence of Tamil genius,' writes the well-known Indian poet, philologist and scholar A.K. Ramanujan on Sangam literature.[4]

Sangam literature is unique and important, as its poems are completely free from Brahmanical diktats and the complex mythical allusions that were the mainstay of Sanskrit literature in the North. There are no stories or myths about gods and goddesses, no philosophical ponderings, no moral dogma; these poems have nothing religious or devout about them and deal with two main subjects: love (*akam*) and war (*puram*). Akam poems deal with the themes of love and lust while puram verses are usually about war and valour, dedicated to kings.

Written in old Tamil, devoid of Aryan influences, they document vivid vignettes of life in South India. These are a collection of verses produced during three literary congregations called *sangam*s, believed to have been composed and compiled between the third century BCE and the third century CE. Collectively, they consist of eight anthologies as well as the Tolkappiyam, a book of grammar and rhetoric. A ninth anthology called the Pattupattu consists of 10 idylls that paint a graphic picture of early Tamil life.

This literature is remarkable for the depth, simplicity and earthiness of its evocative narrative – verses composed by basket weavers, potters, toddy tappers and people who tilled the soil, writing and singing about their everyday lives. Women standing in knee-deep water as they planted paddy sang about errant husbands and cursed their awful mothers-in-law; young girls wrote songs of love and longing; men, about valour and their loyalty to their chieftain. These verses describe their hopes and ambitions, likes and dislikes, traditions and rituals, food habits and, just as importantly, what they drank.

Unlike in the North, where alcohol was restricted to religious ceremonies and Vedic yagnas and was the domain of Brahmin priests, in the South, kings and aristocrats, ordinary men and women, traders, sailors and people who tilled the soil all had easy access to liquor. The Sangam poems, according to well-known translator of Tamil literature George Hart III, are, 'soaked through with toddy'. According to him, almost one in every four poems has one of the words 'toddy' or 'liquor' in it. He writes, 'the warrior king is forever indulging in his favourite toddy made from palm, mahua flowers and other fruits. It is regularly drunk before battles and to fight off shivers and chills.'[5]

> In every settlement, in the huts roofed with grass, they share the clarified toddy that has been buried and matured in liquor jars. (Kapilar, *Purananuru*, 120)

> Mountain dwellers living in huts with narrow eaves drink aged liquor and perform kuravai dances in the front yards of their houses near Vengai trees. (Uraiyur Enicheri Mudamosiyar, *Purananuru*, 129)

> Women too were enthusiastic drinkers:
> A woman who drinks strong liquor swarmed by bees
> Whose eyes used to look like Neythal flowers
> Now resemble the strong reddish Naravan flowers.
> (Paripaatal, 'Euology on Vaiyai', 65–66)[6]

Athiyaman Neduman Anji was one of the most powerful kings of the Sangam era who ruled over a great dynasty called the Cheras. A famous personage in his court was the much-revered Tamil Bhakti poetess called Avvaiyar, whose works are included in the Purananuru. A patron of the arts and literature, Anji was so taken by the earthy wisdom of Avvaiyar that they soon became close friends. A woman who lived her life with wild abandon, 40 of her 52 poems have references to toddy. Perhaps the image of a single woman, bold and wise, might have irked some people of the time, leading to her later-day depiction as an old woman. She writes, 'Toddy drinking by women is part of the daily ritual.'[7] Avvaiyar's poems describe her patron's prowess at war, his feats and strength in the battlefield. She also describes in detail the various cuisines and the taste of the rich meats and strong liquors served in his court. Upon the death of her patron and friend, she glorifies him in a very well-known epitaph where she extols his magnanimity:

> If he had a little toddy, he would give it to us. Alas, not any longer.
>
> If he had abundant toddy, he would give it to us and happily drink the leftover. (Avvaiyar, *Purananuru*, 235)[8]

Further lines allude to the fond relationship between the king and poetess, referring to them sharing *kal*, as alcohol continues to be known in Tamil. She warns

Poruttu Elini, her patron's son, that 'aged toddy is as strong as the sting of a scorpion' (*Purananuru*, 392).[9]

Avvaiyar also refers to the king's generosity, writing that he would happily share his liquor with his valiant warriors:

> The king gathers around him his warriors who imbibe much toddy served in vessels made of leaves. (Avvaiyar, *Pattupattu*, 3)

> After drinking the warrior king becomes more generous with his gifts and a shared drink is regarded as a sign of bonding. (Avvaiyar, *Pattupattu*, 290)[10]

Class divisions disappear here where a courageous and bold warrior refers to the drink kalangal, probably a strong cocktail, offered to him by the king, who himself partakes of the inferior, less potent and plain drink. There are also many verses that sing paeans of praise of their chieftains and kings:

> May you perform fine rituals like your ancestors who received knowledge from teachers of ancient tradition, in whose reign in this fine big city, liquor was filtered in all the fields, dishes were cooked with

> roasted fatty meat and ghee as smoke rose appearing like spreading rain clouds. May you enjoy the good life that has been given to you, being served liquor in gold cups by young women with glittering jewellery.[11]

Another long Tamil poem called 'Malaipatukatam' in the Pattuppattu anthology describes in vivid detail peripatetic drama troupes, dancers and singers who are accorded a warm welcome in every village they visit. It describes the sumptuous food that they are served with large servings of alcohol. Drinking was thus an acceptable social construct, with alcohol being freely consumed by both men and women at weddings, social gatherings, festivals, religious ceremonies, and especially the orgy of *undattu* (which is variously translated as 'dramatic performances', 'festivities' and 'drinking binges') that often followed battle victories. Also, unlike the North, the South was more egalitarian when it came to alcohol – there were no caste distinctions, the same liquor being available to all castes and classes. Drinking, needless to say, was prevalent among the royals, chieftains, landlords – zamindars and feudal – as well as all visitors and guests. In one verse, irrespective of her father being drunk, a 'dutiful' daughter offers him a glass of liquor along with the viraal fish she has cooked for him. 'Not for nothing do two primary terms for happiness in Tamil, *kali* and *magizhchi*, have their etymology in drinking,' writes the renowned historian, author, translator and professor A.R. Venkatachalapathy.[12]

The use of alcohol was so ubiquitous that the Pallava king Mahendravarman I (590–630 CE), under whose tutelage South India became a major political power, took note of the impunity with which people drank – even those for whom it was prohibited, including many a monk as Buddhism and Jainism held sway in Tamil Nadu for several centuries.

Mahendravarman was a man of many accomplishments, known for his literary skills, the huge temples he built, his proficiency in playing the veena as well as other creative activities like dramaturgy, painting and music. He is also credited with having written one of the first satires in Indian literature, called *Mattavilasa Prahasana* ('Addicted to Pleasure'). Using alcohol as a metaphor, he explores the hypocrisies of the various monistic religious sects.

The play, set in Kanchipuram, the Pallava capital city, derides the hypocrisy of various religious groups of the time who flouted their scriptural tenets with impunity. It opens with two drunken Kapalikas called Satyasoma and his woman, Devasoma, who go bar-hopping in search of alcohol. The Kapalikas are followers of a heretic Saivite sect whose rituals include drinking, wild dancing, singing and ritual intercourse with their partners. After the drinking binge, as per tradition, Satyasoma sets out to seek *bhiksha* or alms when he realizes that he has lost his sacred skull begging bowl. The couple set out in search of the bowl and come across a Buddhist monk, Nagasena, whom they accuse of stealing their bowl. They say that Buddhist monks steal, lie, drink liquor, eat meat and womanize even though their religion prohibits them to. The heated argument predictably leads to a brawl. As the fighting escalates, another mendicant comes to mediate when, suddenly, a madman comes holding Satyasoma's skull bowl, saying he had retrieved it from a dog.

The play describes life in Kanchipuram – the vibrant city life, the fragrant flower shops, the festive climate within its many taverns – and also alludes to the corrupt courts where officials were easily bribed. It was against the backdrop of Hindu synthesis, a movement of the emergence of devotional sects and a resurgence of brahminical influence that attempted to bring back

Jains and Buddhists into the Hindu fold, that this satire was written.

Tamilakam was the name that was used to refer to the entire territory of South India, comprising the present states of Andhra Pradesh, Karnataka, Kerala and Tamil Nadu as well as parts of Sri Lanka. Historians usually refer to the 'whole of the Ancient Tamil country' as a single geographic area, though many different kingdoms co-existed within its boundaries. This Dravida country, though viewed as a homogenous entity, had distinctively different landscapes, distinct linguistic communities as well as separate cultural and religious traditions, carving out separate identities for themselves. Ruled from the third century BCE by various dynasties, here the arts, music, architecture and literature flourished. Telugu, Kannada and Malayalam evolved into separate languages known for their literary excellence. These regions also developed their own traditions, cultures, cuisines and beliefs. But what was common to the whole region was what they drank.

If the people of Tamil country expressed their penchant for alcohol in verse, their neighbours in Karnataka literally etched it in stone. In the third century BCE, the whole region came under the influence of Buddhism and Jainism under the tutelage of Emperor Chandragupta Maurya, who had fled south due a severe famine in North India. By the third century CE, Buddhism started losing its grip, chiefly due to loss of royal patronage, which was further aided by the efforts to revive Hinduism. As the influence of Jainism and Buddhism started to wane, people very soon reverted to ways that were familiar to them.

Brewing and drinking was considered to be an art all over ancient India and Karnataka was no exception. Sculptures, wall paintings and inscriptions bear witness to the fact that drinking was quite commonplace. Many Kannada *kavya*s (literary masterpieces) give picturesque descriptions of taverns and drinking rituals, attesting that drinking was prevalent, a social and often communal affair that provided amusement and relief after a hard day at the fields.

*Manasollasa* ('Happiness of the Mind'), also known as *Abhilashitartha Chintamani*, is yet another early twelfth-century Sanskrit text composed by the Chalukyan king Someshvara III. It is an encyclopaedic work that covers topics such as ethics, economics, astronomy, astrology, veterinary medicine, horticulture, perfumes, architecture, painting, poetry and music.

It is however best known as an invaluable source of sociocultural information on twelfth-century South India, particularly as a source guide for food, drinks and cuisines – a work that precedes all the cookbooks in Europe by over a century. While the text is not the first among Indian books to describe fermented foods, it contains a range of cuisines based on fermented cereals and flour and has lengthy descriptions of flavoured waters and fruit drinks called *panaka*s. Along with food, the fine art of wine-making finds pride of place. As the climate of Karnataka was more congenial than that of its neighbours, grapes were grown there, leading to large-scale wine production.

Karnataka is home to a variety of uniquely flavoured indigenous alcohols and liquors. Strong liquors were distilled from rice and ragi, grapes, mangoes, jackfruit and dates flavoured with flower essences. Some brews were so strong that Kalhana, the celebrated twelfth-century poet-historian from Kashmir, in his magnum opus *Rajatarangini*, makes special mention of the fact that the soldiers of King Lalitadya, who had marched south on a conquering spree, were used to milder wines made from grapes flavoured with saffron. These soldiers, on reaching the banks of the Kaveri River, had their first taste of the much stronger palm toddy and other sweet-sour foamy drinks that, says the text, made the Kashmiri soldiers more than happy and inebriated for sure!

Drinking, though commonplace, was a serious undertaking, to be practised with ritual and ceremony in a pleasant environment. First the goddess of wine (Madhu Devate) was invoked, and then Mother Earth was propitiated. As everything that was consumed was first offered to the gods, liquor too was ritually sprinkled all around first before being consumed. It was then poured into artistically shaped bowls with bird heads, carved from mother of pearl, beautiful shells, ivory, silver and gold. Older members of the family and community were first offered the liquor and only then were younger people allowed to pour themselves a drink. Married couples, family members, friends and relatives all joined these drinking sessions. It was equally common for women to have a drink or two while they gossiped. Snacks were also served with the drinks as well as a dose of ghee and *kashayam* (a herbal drink) to avoid the effects of inebriation.[13]

Kanakadasa, the well-known fifteenth-century saint-poet and a towering figure in Kannada literature, wrote the *Mohanatarangini*, a composition in verse that narrates various tales from the Puranas as well as life in Krishna's Dwarka. He vividly describes marketplaces with colourful stalls and demarcated lanes teeming with craftsmen, clients and merchants; royal garden parties and glorious descriptions of the palace, all reminiscent of the fabulous Vijayanagara empire under Krishnadevaraya. Known as the golden age, life under the Raya king was prosperous, stable, opulent and egalitarian.

A description of a drinking bout with men and women of the working classes is particularly vivid:

Drink, the celestial beauty!
Drink my golden doll,
Drink the moon-faced, curly haired mate.

Drink my heartthrob,
Drink the civilized one,
Drink my Handsome.
I can't go on if you stop![14]

Karnataka is resplendent with a number of exquisitely sculpted temples, which were not just places of worship but also a holistic part of the community, places that symbolically brought man and God and man and man together. Their large halls were places for social, economic and political interaction, where people gathered every day to worship as well as exchange news. The temple walls and panels, pillars and ceilings are all sculpted not just with tales of gods and goddesses but with scenes from everyday lives – processions where the king is followed by his chieftains on horses, festive parades with men and women dancing, singing and playing various musical instruments. Drinking too finds pride of place in these sculptures, showing that it was acceptable enough to be depicted even on temple walls – there are market scenes, depictions of men in taverns and bars and scenes in bazaars. Sculptures in the third cave at Badami depict an inebriated young man giving a lecture on temperance and couples fighting over goblets of wine while servants stand respectfully behind them holding jugs to replenish their cups.[15] There are depictions of inebriated women who have lost control over their body and clothing being carried off.

In a temple in Kolar, the presiding deity Kolaramma is shown holding a goblet in her hand, and there is an inscription giving grants to make *mattiya pana* (liquor). In the Khetappayya Narayana temple in Bhatkal, there are sculptures of couples drinking. The ceiling of the Narasimhaswamy Temple in Sibi is painted with elaborate scenes of toddy tapping: a man atop a palm tree is collecting the toddy in pots while a woman is shown pouring the collected toddy from the pots into a leather bag. A third person readies to transport it on a donkey. All of these were obviously very common scenes from everyday life.

The magnificent capital city of the Raya kings, Vijayanagara, was one of the greatest metropolises of India – in fact, of the entire medieval world. Located on the banks of the Tungabhadra River, it carried on a brisk trade in rubies, pearls and diamonds from the nearby Golconda mines, importing mercury, Chinese silks and wines. Domingo Paes, the Portuguese traveller, says, 'What I saw from thence [a hill] seemed to me as large as Rome, and very beautiful to the sight; there are many lakes, groves of trees within it, in the gardens of the houses [...] and the king has close to his palace a palm-grove and other rich-bearing fruit-trees.'[16] Despite being known for its proficiency in trade and the king's interest in the arts, it was a war economy, therefore, taxes were imposed on homes, shops, salt, toddy, toddy tappers and even prostitutes.

The neighbouring Kakatiya kings were similar and just as prosperous, located as they were along the fertile Godavari and Krishna river basins. They too carried on brisk trade with other countries, operated through well-organized *srenis* or guilds. All manner of merchants and artisans had their own guilds; epigraphs refer to guilds of weavers, agriculturists, oil pressers, toddy tappers, mat makers, goldsmiths, potters and jewellers. Marco Polo, the Italian mercantile trader-explorer who arrived in India between 1292 and 1294, visited Motupalli, the main port of the Kakatiyas, and noted the vigorous trade in a variety of items, including scents such as sandal, camphor and rose water; ivory, pearls and corals; a range of metals like copper, zinc and lead; silk, pepper, wine and areca nuts.

Not to be left behind is Kerala, which was an integral part of Tamilakam, differentiated here because it is a different state today. Ruled by Chera kings who transformed Kerala into an international trade centre, it was, with its natural beauty, a land blessed with plenitude – spices of every kind had drawn people to its shores for thousands of years (for instance, pepper was found stuffed up the nose of the 3,000-year-old mummy of the Egyptian Pharaoh Ramses II). Lush forests which yielded timber that was used to build the sixth-century BCE Sumerian Ziggurat of Ur in Mesopotamia, undulating paddy fields, magnificent backwaters and swaying coconut and palm trees –

Kerala has always been God's country.

'With its streets, its houses, its covered fishing boats, where they sell fish, where they pile up rice ... where the sacks of pepper are heaped up – with its gold deliveries, carried by ocean-going ships and brought to the river bank by local boats, ... the city that bestows wealth to its visitors ... the city where liquor abounds, yes, this [Muziris] ... is given to me like a marvel, a treasure,' says the Purananuru of the historical port-city of Muziris in Kerala.[17]

Medieval travellers who travelled to the Malabar Coast were astounded by the wealth, grandeur, sophistication and secular lives that people lived. Centuries of exposure and interlinking with foreigners had turned the locals into a cosmopolitan tolerant people, accustomed to different languages and customs. Kerala has always been a secular land, assimilating the Romans and Greeks who came in their big ships, Arab travellers who came in their dhows and the subsequent armadas of the Portuguese, Dutch, French and English. Trade and wealth aside, these foreigners were also surprised at the enlightened level of governance, freedom, secularism and the royal patronage of the arts.

Religious freedom was a given, and one such personal folk deity still worshipped in Kerala and around Coorg in Karnataka is Muthappan, an amalgam of Siva and Vishnu. Practices in these Muthappan temples are quite distinct from the rather rigid norms followed in other Hindu places of worship; these temples are also open to everyone irrespective of caste, creed and community. The idol is worshipped with offerings of *madyam* (toddy) and *mamsam* (flesh-fish). As usual, there are attendant mythologies associated with the Muthappan deity. The story goes that the ruler of Eruvessi, being childless, prayed to Siva. The queen, while returning after bathing in the river one day, saw a pretty child lying on a nearby rock. She took the child home, and the couple raised him as their own son. Growing up, the boy went into the nearby jungles to hunt, always giving food to the poor and mingling with everyone irrespective of caste or creed. This was unacceptable behaviour for a prince, and his parents sternly forbade him from it and threatened him with dire consequences. The boy then showed his parents his true divine form as the all-pervading Lord.

He, however, decided to leave the palace and, on his travels, became greatly drawn to toddy from the palm trees. Soon, a local toddy tapper, Chandan, realized that his toddy was being stolen and decided to guard the palm trees, only to discover that the thief was an old man. Greatly angered, he set out to shoot the old man but instead fell down and became unconscious. Heartbroken thinking her husband had died, Chandan's wife started wailing but, looking heavenwards, saw the old man perched atop the palm tree. Calling him 'Muthappan' ('Muthappan' means 'grandfather' in Malayalam), she sought his help while praying to God to save her husband; and sure enough, Chandan regained consciousness. Grateful, she fed the old man boiled gram, fish and large quantities of toddy, which pleased Muthappan immensely.

In yet another interesting tale associated with the Nileshwar Muthappan Madappura Temple, an elderly scholar from a distinguished local family used to regularly visit a spot where he would enjoy a quiet moment and have a glass or two of madhu, the local toddy. Before drinking, he would sprinkle a few drops of the liquor on the nearby jackfruit tree as an offering to the god Muthappan. This became a daily ritual until he died. On his passing, the villagers started experiencing serious issues in the village. On consulting a soothsayer, they were told that the cause of their troubles was because Lord Muthappan, who until then had been receiving regular tots of liquor, had moved away since there was no one now to give him his daily drink. The natives immediately erected a Muthappan temple there, where the offering was obviously toddy.

Some of the vestiges that have survived from pre-Vedic times are the local protective gods. Villages across India have guardian gods called *grama devata*s, though they are more prevalent in South India. All the southern states have their own version of these folk deities who protect their villages. These deities are, to a large part, women who understand and safeguard the needs of the locals. Called *amman* or 'mother', these rural goddesses are seen as maternal protectors, fierce and strong, powerful warriors, protectors from calamities like floods and famine and destroyers of disease like smallpox. The goddesses are worshiped by people from all castes; daily rituals and festivals are usually performed and celebrated by toddy sellers.

In the villages of Tamil Nadu, Andhra Pradesh, Karnataka and even Kerala, one also finds *kaval daivam* – male deities or attendants to the female deities. They are believed to guard the shrines and carry out the commands of these goddesses. Gigantic statues of these male deities with wide-open horrifying large eyes, a long, protruding tongue, holding weapons like *aruval* (sword) and *sangili* (iron chain), mounted on a white horse and with a *veetai nayi* (hunting dog) beside them, these deities are ritually offered packs of cigarettes and bottles of alcohol to enable them to do their jobs properly!

Although emerging from a common template, all four states have developed distinctly different features observed in the manner in which people communicate, socialize, worship and eat. But while much seems different, the basics remain the same. All four states are blessed with long, undulating coastlines and tropical climates ideal for growing all manner of palms and coconuts, so ubiquitous that they are cultural icons of the tropics. Indeed, the palmyra has been the official tree of Tamil country for many a century.

The coconut derives its name from the sixteenth-century Portuguese and Spanish word *coco*, which means 'head' or 'skull', because of the three indentations on the coconut shell that resemble a pair of human eyes and nose. Known as the tree of life, it is one of the trees most put to work in the world, where every bit of it is used to provide nutrition, shelter, sustenance, jobs, medicine and liquor. Manuscripts were made out of dried palm leaves and used as writing material dating as far back as the fifth century BCE; the leaves were used to thatch roofs of houses and weave baskets; the stalks were used to make picket fences; split trunks were used as roof joists; the oil was used for cooking, the husks, for ropes and the sticks, for brooms. The flesh of the fruit provided food, and the water and sap, irresistible alcohol. A Tamil proverb ascribes to the palm '801 kinds of uses, meeting almost all the needs of a man'.

The exact origin and genesis of toddy is not known, but it has been made and used for as long as there have been men. Wherever there are coconut or palm trees, one can safely assume that alcohol is being brewed. There is an oft-repeated saying in Tamil: '*Pana marathadiyil thanner kudithhalum, kallu yena nenaipparkal*,' meaning, 'If you drink even plain water standing beneath a palm tree, it will be assumed that you drink *kallu*.'

Variously known as *taadi* and *sendi* in Kannada, *thati kallu* in Telugu and kallu in Tamil and Malayalam, it is classified and sold in two sizes, large and small. The process of making toddy consists of several stages. When fresh sap is collected from incising coconut clusters, it is known as *neera*, which is a sweet and non-alcoholic beverage. When fermented, it becomes palm wine; when distilled, it is known as arrack – what foreigners referred to as 'coconut vodka' – a drink much favoured by sailors. When this sap is left to ferment for a short while, it is known as kallu. These trees are precious but also highly productive, each one capable of producing over 300 litres of toddy per year. With South India accounting for over 70 per cent of the seven-to-eight crore trees, that's certainly a lot of alcohol being generated.

Calling it a 'capital drink', Marco Polo again observed how 'this wine is drawn from trees':

> Wine is not made; but from a species of tree resembling the date-bearing palm they procure an excellent beverage .... They cut off a branch, and put over the place a vessel to receive the juice as it distils from the wound, which is filled in the course of a day and a night. So wholesome are the qualities of this liquor, that it affords relief in dropsical complaints, as well as in those of the lungs and of the spleen.[18]

Being an integral part of the traditions and culture in the South, alcohol is used in wedding ceremonies – the groom, when going to his in-laws' house, is supposed to carry previously negotiated quantities of palm wine. Rituals like small amounts of toddy being sprinkled all around oneself is a practice that is followed by men before they sit down for their drinking sessions. Accounts from the eighteenth century describe workers and landowners sharing a drink after work – unthinkable in more caste-bound regions. There are many stories about 'toddy buddies', boisterous men after major religious festivals where drinking was de rigueur and wealthy 'minors' (zamindars) who surveyed their lands, 'debauched and prone to eating meat and drinking strong liquors'. Women, though not as visibly, drank too, often getting together over gossip sessions. Palm wine was offered to guests at weddings, birth celebrations as well as funerals. It continues to be used in cuisine too, as a leavening agent in many a South Indian dish like appam, idli and dosa.

Indians also knew about the anaesthetic effect of alcohol, and it was freely available on the battlefield when wounded soldiers needed relief from excruciating pain. According to Xuanzang, the Chinese pilgrim (639 CE), sharp swords were tied to the trunks of inebriated elephants and let loose on enemy battalions. The havoc and ensuing chaos must have been terrible, but the soldiers, fed on large quantities of alcohol, fought on mindlessly without fear. It also continues to be used in medicine in tinctures, as a sedative and as a mild laxative, and is good for weak stomachs.

Duarte Barbosa, the Portuguese voyager who spent 16 years in India, most of them in Kerala, wrote in *Book of Duarte Barbosa* that indulgence in liquors may not have been considered respectable but was very common among the Nairs, describing them as being 'excessively addicted to intoxicating liquors'. But good times do not last forever, and by the time the Pallavas came to power (275–897 CE), there were levies imposed, ironically not on the liquor itself but on the toddy tappers, called *ezha poochi* or *ezha pattam*.

In the centuries following the Sangam era, there was a marked attitudinal shift towards alcohol. Thiruvalluvar (500 CE), the celebrated Tamil poet and philosopher, is best known for his work the Thirukkural, a collection of couplets on ethics, politics and economy, relationships and society. The text, much revered by Tamils even today, advocated not for temperance but for abstinence, with many a verse on the ill effects of alcohol on families and economies:

> Consume not alcohol; consume if you will,
> those who care not to be held highly by the noble.
> (922)
>
> They have no sense of consequences,
> Those who pay to lose their senses.
> One who is asleep is no different from the dead;
> one who consumes alcohol forever consumes
> poison. (926)

Those who are in a perpetual drunken stupor
shall be sneered at by the knowing locals. (927)

Drunken revelry is horrid in front of your mother;
how would it seem in front of the esteemed? (933)

The good lady, Sense of Shame, will turn her back on
those despicably guilty of being drunk. (934)[19]

The extent of consumption of local liquors led the British to immediately set up a tax on liquor both locally brewed and imported, creating havoc among tribal communities. And as the nationalist movement for Indian independence grew, Tamil Nadu grew more and more moralistic, spearheaded by C. Rajagopalachari, statesman, writer, lawyer and activist as well as the last governor-general of India, who became one of the strongest champions of Mahatma Gandhi's call for prohibition.

In 1986, the unexpected happened. Ironically, the first state to not just breach prohibition but open its doors to independent bars and pubs was none other than Bengaluru, a city that until then had gone to sleep at 9.00 p.m. Suddenly the town came alive with a hitherto unknown nightlife and, coupled with the tech revolution, became India's answer to Silicon Valley, abuzz with a young cosmopolitan working and drinking population.

In the interim, Andhra Pradesh and Kerala continued to drink undeterred. Endowed with nature's bounty, it is hardly surprising that two of the four southern states, Andhra Pradesh and Kerala, top the list of the highest consumers of local alcohol in the country.[20]

It is the ambivalence of centuries of easy availability with uncensored enjoyment of alcohol and the subsequent shrill rhetoric about the ills of excessive drinking as propagated by reformers and politicians that lies at the heart of the recurring cycles of prohibition in South India. Despite its liberal and egalitarian traditions in the past, Tamil Nadu has been most prone to prohibition while the other three states continue to alternate between political compulsions and financial necessities.

# 4

# Mughal Majesty: Hedonism and Piety

The seventh century saw the rise of Islam, and the ensuing invasions by Muslim leaders transformed the socio-religio-political landscape across much of the world, including India. Marauding tribes, looting, rape, conversion and coercion became commonplace in South Asia as some of the conquering invaders set up various dynasties in the subcontinent.

The advent of the Mughals in the sixteenth century altered India irrevocably. Ruthless warlords, they ironically had a finely developed sense of aesthetics, influenced as they were by the Persians. Under their rule, food, clothing, art, poetry, music, religion, everything changed. Surrounded by opulence and known for their love of the arts and architecture, they were connoisseurs of the finer aspects of life, and though forbidden to consume opiates and alcohol as Muslims, their courts overflowed with wine and song.

Drugs, alcohol and sex feature prominently during the reigns of the first six Mughal emperors.

A popular saying of those times goes as follows:

Only the drinker knows the pleasure of wine.
What enjoyment thereof can the sober have?

A sentiment that the Mughal emperors wholeheartedly endorsed.

Islam has some 1.2 billion followers today, making it the world's second-largest religion and the one that has spread the fastest. From 655 CE, spanning some 1,400 years, Muslim conquests following the death of Prophet Muhammad led to the creation of caliphates that began to occupy vast swathes of land through conquest and conversion.

India had already been trading with the seafaring Arab world for over 800 years along the Coromandel and Gujarat coasts. When the religion originated, Islam gained early acceptance among these traders, as they had had centuries of profitable and reliable interaction with Arabia. The first three mosques in India were in fact set up in Tamil Nadu, Kerala and Gujarat as early as 630 CE.

Islam arrived in the hinterland in the seventh century, when Muslims invaded from the northwest. The first Muslim invasion of India, led by Muhammad Bin Qasim in 711 CE, resulted in the conquest of Sindh. This was followed in rapid succession by invasions and looting sprees by the likes of Mahmud of Ghazni (who plundered India 17 times), Qutb al-Din Aibak as well as Muhammad Ghori, subsequently paving the way for several sultanates that sprang in the subcontinent, all of either Turkic or Afghan origin, such as the Mamluks, Khaljis, Tughlaqs, Sayyids and Lodis.

These five dynasties ruled India for over 320 years and, at their height, occupied much of the Indian subcontinent. These invasions were different as, unlike the previous invaders who assimilated into the prevalent social system, the Muslim conquerors retained their new Islamic identity and created social systems that challenged and superimposed Islamic tenets onto existing traditions. These new cultural idioms created a hybrid culture vastly different from what had, up until then, been largely Hindu traditions.

Society under the Delhi Sultanate had a hierarchy and was broadly divided into the aristocracy, priests, townsmen and peasants. Noblemen, mostly Muslims, lived a life of luxury and enjoyed prominent positions in the courts, acting as administrators, generals and oftentimes even king makers. The power of these nobles was inversely proportionate to the power of the kings, growing stronger as the kings became weaker.

Among these dissolute nobles, drinking and gambling became a way of life, often leading to administrative lapses and invasions. For example, Sultan Firuz Shah Tughlaq who succeeded his cousin Muhammad bin Tughlaq observed religious injunction with utmost devotion but enjoyed drinking secretly; on one occasion, in the midst of a campaign he was caught by his army commander Tatar Khan lying half naked in bed surrounded by wine cups and was reproached for this depravity.

Alauddin Khilji, a powerful sultan from the Khilji dynasty, is best known for fending off the invading Mongols and establishing a consolidated power. Seeing the dissipation of the nobles around him, he undertook large-scale reforms prohibiting the sale and use of liquor and intoxicants in Delhi and surrounding areas, forbade parties and marriages among the nobles without his permission, confiscated *jagir*s and estates, and stopped pensions and allowances for those who did not fall in line. In an attempt to set an example, he himself gave up drinking. Alas, it was all in vain – the court and the general public continued to eat and drink as they deemed fit, and after his death, the overindulgence and dissolute behaviour of the aristocracy only worsened.

The waning power of the Delhi Sultanate was further weakened by invasion in 1398 by the Turkic Mongol conqueror Timur, also known as Timurlane, who ransacked Delhi, leaving behind utter wreckage and destruction. The subsequent dynasties rapidly got reduced to being mere provisional principalities – with the exception of the Lodis, who hailed from Afghanistan. India, however, had not seen the last of Timur, whose successors went on to establish two significant empires: one in Central Asia and Persia known as the Timurid dynasty, and the other in the Indian subcontinent.

Descendants of two great Central Asian conquerors – Genghis Khan, founder of the Mongol Dynasty, and Timur – the first Mughal rulers followed the familiar pattern of adventurous chieftains from the mountains in the northwest, attracted by visions of wealth and power, sensing a period of internal weakness, gathering forces and descending upon the fertile plains of the

Punjab. Among these was Babur who, convinced that he would not meet with too much resistance, marched into Lahore; his subsequent victory against Ibrahim Lodi opened the gates to the Indian subcontinent. Soon he was the master of the entire Indo-Gangetic Plain, Herat in Afghanistan, the Punjab as well as a long line of forts all over Central India.

The stage was set for the rise of the Mughal Empire.

Babur, ironically, did not like being known as a Mongol, as this evoked memories of Genghis Khan's massacres. Unfortunately, though, he and his descendants would carry forward those Mongolian genes – tribes who were known just as much for their barbaric violence as they were for their intimate encounters with alcohol.

The Mongols were hard drinking, barbaric and ruthless warriors not given to much finesse or decorum. 'Consuming huge quantities of alcohol was a major pastime of the Mongol elite with the most popular tipple from the Great Khans to lowly shepherds being fermented mare's milk' known as *airag* or *kumis*.[1]

Drinking alcohol was a very important part of Mongolian culture – both men and women were encouraged to drink to the beat of a drum or clapping hands at festivals, weddings and ceremonies. Besides kumis, other alcoholic drinks included honey wine, known as *boal*, but as their empire expanded, the Mongols soon got exposed to stronger alternatives. Beer, wine from grapes or rice, and other types of distilled liquor were consumed in vast quantities, with the ability to drink worn as a badge of honour. It was not without its downside, though, with the early deaths of several Mongol leaders being attributed to alcohol.

The emergence of Islam threw into disarray the tribal Arabs who until then had always been partial to alcohol. 'Wine was very common in Arabia before Islam.'[2] Some modern authors maintain that there are approximately a thousand words for wine in Arabic, while others claim there are a 'mere 250'. Interestingly the word 'araku', which is used for liquor throughout Tamil Nadu, has its genesis in Arabic. 'Arak' is an Arabic word that loosely translates as sweat, probably referring to the condensation while brewing. The word is used extensively in south Asia for a variety of locally made liquors.

Needless to say, alcohol was top of mind recall in Arabia. There were several books written about wine by Arab authors, for example the *Qutb as-surur fi wasf al-anbad wal-humur* written by Abu Ishaq al-Katib al-Qairawani.[3]

And then came Islam – from the earliest days, there was much confusion about the drinking decree. Were Muslims to completely abjure from drinking or were certain kinds of drinks permitted? Was there a restriction on the amount of alcohol to be consumed? What would be the penalties if people drank? Like much else, the jury was divided on this. However inflexible and dogmatic religious diktats may be, people have an ability to improvise, interpreting them situationally to suit their own convenience and habits. Flexibility was by no means unique nor restricted only to the Mughals, who found a convenient way out.

Historian, professor and author Stephanie Honchell explains in her dissertation:

> Hanafi scholars formed one of four traditional Sunni schools; they were interpreters of Islamic jurisprudence and settled in Iraq, the Ottoman empire as well as in the Indian sub-continent. These scholars while upholding the unlawfulness of intoxication restricted its definition to fermented juice of grapes or dates. As a result, alcohol made from other means such as honey, barley, wheat and millet like whisky, beer and vodka was permitted although all forms of grape alcohol were completely banned.[4]

That resolved one problem. So, if only wine from grapes was banned, was there a restriction on quantity? Averroes, a twelfth-century Muslim Andalusian polymath and jurist, explains in his encyclopaedia of comparative Islamic jurisprudence:

> In their argument by way of reasoning they said that the Koran has explicitly laid down that the *Illa* (underlying cause) of prohibition of *khamr* (wine) is that it prevents the remembrance of God and breeds enmity and hatred ... [this is] found only in a certain quantity of the intoxicating liquor not in what is less than that; it follows therefore that only this quantity be prohibited.[5]

Then there remained the vexing question of quantum of punishment if there were transgressions. Hanafi jurists delineated drinking-related offences into two categories:

1. Drinking grape-derived wine known as khamr (punishment applicable on drinking 'even a drop')[6]
2. Intoxication from non-grape intoxicants (certainly prohibited from a religious-moral perspective, but may or may not qualify for criminal punishment)

The second category of punishment was specific to the Hanafis as other schools punished drinking regardless of the level of intoxication; as such, they had to come up with a legal definition of drunkenness. So, they defined a drunk as he 'whose intellect has left him so he does not understand a little or much (of anything at all)' or he who 'does not know (the difference) between a man and a woman or the earth from the sky'.[7]

While all other schools of Islamic jurisprudence completely prohibited the consumption of alcohol in all forms, the Hanafi understanding of Shariah permitted adherents not only to indulge in alcoholic beverages but to do so up to a near point of total 'annihilation'.[8]

However, by the twelfth century, the Hanafi school too embraced the prohibition of all alcohol and fell in line with the other schools.[9]

Not that the ensuing strict injunctions made by Islamic jurisprudence made much difference, especially to the rulers of Persia, Afghanistan and India. Though their Mongolian ancestry would come repeatedly to haunt their dynasty, Babur took pride in his Timurid connections. The Mughal dynasty was essentially Turkish, and Timur's court at the magnificent city of Samarkand would attract numerous scholars, poets, musicians and philosophers. This was the environment that Babur had grown up in, and he and his successors strived to transplant these cultural traditions into Lahore, Delhi and Agra. Their continued rule for over 300 years provided dynastic stability and contributed to a rich and varied cultural life that can be seen in every aspect of Indian life today. Babur himself was a writer of great distinction, and his autobiography, the *Baburnama*, is considered one of the finest works of Turkish prose.

The *Baburnama* is a candid autobiography in which Babur expresses nostalgia for his homeland, clearly not enamoured with the lands he has conquered. Women, too, don't seem to interest him much, though he married several times and had numerous children. He is extremely forthright about his relationship with alcohol, starting with the drinking habits of his father, Umar Shaikh Mirza II, whom he recalls drank a lot, held drinking parties at least once or twice a week, had an affinity for an intoxicating confection called *ma'jun* and was an avid gambler. The drinking was not restricted to his father; of his three brothers, he appears to be the only one whose health was not compromised by alcohol. Babur's brother Sultan Nasir

Mirza, who was in charge of Kabul, died as a result of overindulgence.

The poet Mirza Haidar cites the following verse to describe the young prince's affliction:

> Every time my heart is pained by a hangover,
> I quaff so much wine that my body ceases to exist.
> (30)[10]

Babur's relationship with alcohol, because it is so extensively documented in his own words, appears to be complex and extreme, swinging from excessive indulgence to guilt leading to abstinence. His drinking habits changed and evolved significantly over the course of his life, reflecting his own growth from a small-time Timurid prince to becoming the founder of a very significant South Asian empire.

The birth of the empire was celebrated with a raucous drinking party. Babur makes a passing reference to the party, stating that he returned to the camp and drank spirits (*araq*) on a boat; his companion Shaikh Zain Khwafi, who held the position of Sadr chief justice and wrote a Persian recension of portions of the *Baburnama*, records it with a bit more flair, in verse:

The diver of his heart in the waves of the sea of wine
Plunged and drew out the measuring rope from the froth of reason;
The king who had subdued the whole world
Was himself vanquished in a moment by the world of a drinking bout.[11]

Babur says he only started drinking when he was about 30, and although religion occupied centre stage in his life, he quotes a verse by one of his contemporaries: 'I am drunk, officer. Punish me when I am sober.' He writes that his nights were filled with drunken carousing and is described by his cousin and admirer Mirza Haidar Dughlat as a person who drank 'religiously'. His drinking bouts were legendary.

In one of the first stories in the *Baburnama*, he admits to blacking out and drunkenly riding his horse through camp, an event that has been immortalized in a painting commissioned by his grandson Akbar. In another instance, Babur had just returned to Kabul and decided to host a party at the outskirts of the city. He and his companions drank so much that some of them had difficulty mounting their horses at the end of the evening, even with the help of their servants. One man in particular, Dost-Muhammad Baqir, was so drunk that his servants could not lift him on to his horse. The light-hearted situation quickly turned dangerous when the group was set upon by a band of Afghans. Still unable to get Dost-Muhammad on his horse, another of the men, the equally intoxicated Amin-Muhammad Tarkhan, jokingly proposed chopping off Dost-Muhammad's head, which they could then carry away, protecting him from the Afghans. Luckily, the servants intervened, managing to put Dost-Muhammad on his horse, and the whole party returned safely to Kabul.[12]

One aspect of the Mongol imperial drinking culture that was described by Ruy Gonzáles de Clavijo, the Spanish ambassador at Timur's court, was the number of high-ranking women who regularly enjoyed wine alongside their male counterparts. This Central Asian culture seems to have been carried forward by Babur's court, where drinking was not an exclusive homosocial activity, until he had an untoward experience.

It is said that Babur once enthusiastically invited a woman called Huhlul Anikä who wanted to join his drinking parties. While the party began well enough, Babur found it impossible to relax because Huhlul Anikä would not stop chatting and started making 'offensive requests'. He finally escaped her by pretending to be drunk and, needless to say, did not make any further attempts to include women in his parties, which eventually led to women getting relegated to their private spaces or zenanas.

This, however, did not change the intellectual capacity of these women or the power that they wielded. Royal women continued to exert considerable influence as political advisors and participants in literary and court matters. Babur's mother and grandmother served as two of his earliest political advisors; later there were Gulbadan Begum, Hamida Banu Begum, Nur Jahan, Jahanara and Zebunnisa, all prominent examples of highly influential royal women.[13]

Babur was entirely unconcerned about appearances and the need for propriety or sobriety for his court or army. He appears to revel in the extremes of his own and others' intoxication. The equanimity with which Babur regarded his own drunkenness is explained when he reveals that he had sworn to renounce drinking when he turned forty and admits to 'drinking to excess out of anxiety'.[14]

Eventually, all excesses take their toll. Faced with the redoubtable Rana Sangram Singh at the historic Battle of Khanwa and staring at the imminent defeat that would cost him his empire, Babur prayed for divine assistance, promising to give up drinking in return. He records the event in the *Baburnama*: 'I sent for all the gold and silver goblets and cups along with all other utensils used for my drinking parties and directed them to be broken and renounced the use of wine, purifying my mind. The broken utensils were distributed among the poor and the *darvesh*.'[15]

Babur was obviously a man with very strong willpower for he never broke his promise, though there were moments of regret. In a letter to his friend Khwaja Kalan he admits to craving for alcohol, ending the letter with a few lines about his struggle to stay committed to his vow of temperance:

> I am distraught to have given up wine.
> I do not know what to do, and I am perplexed.
> Everybody regrets drinking and then takes the oath,
> But I have taken the oath and now regret it.[16]

Even though he gave up drinking, his court continued to host lavish parties and social gatherings, but his sobriety took away any pleasure that he might have previously had, making him slowly withdrew from these celebrations. He writes, 'The craving for a wine party was so overwhelming that many times out of longing for wine I would be on the verge of weeping.'[17] Babur's daughter Gulbadan also mentions her father's strong will to remain sober. She talks about how they had constructed an octagonal pool that they had planned to fill with wine, which after Babur's vow was replaced by lemon sherbet.

Besides his willpower, Babur was also known for his generosity – something that would come back to bite him. He writes how after the victory at Panipat, he distributed the immense Lodi treasury among the citizenry of Kabul. Babur's son Humayun, who had offered protection to members of the Gwalior Raja's family in Agra during the battle, was presented with a 40-gram diamond as a token of their gratitude. There is no clear indication whether this was indeed the fabled Kohinoor, though. Humayun gave it to his father, who returned it without a second thought. This and other acts of generosity earned Babur the title of Qalandar, which pleased him immensely.

There were other acts of kindness that he came to regret. Ibrahim Lodi's mother, whom he protected and presented with a large estate, conspired to have him killed by serving him poisoned food and drink. This betrayal by someone whom he had provided sanctuary to and treated with kindness would corrupt the Mughals' dynamics with food and drink far into the future. Babur recovered from this near fatal poisoning, but his health was never the same after this incident.

He died in 1530 in Agra and was succeeded by his son Humayun.[18]

Humayun was 23 when he took over his father's empire – an empire that was far from consolidated. While he had some experience as a military commander, he lacked his father's vigour and toughness and was unable to quell the rising dissatisfaction among his noblemen and army. Succession quarrels with his brothers did not help either; his half-brother Kamran Mirza, who had inherited Kabul and Kandahar, turned into a bitter rival and had also lost much of the Mughal territory to the increasingly powerful Sher Shah Suri in the east and Sultan Bahadur of Gujarat in the west.

Humayun possessed all the humane qualities of his father but lacked 'the decision and spirit of command without which no prince can secure the respect and confidence of his subject'.[19] Excessive opium, another scourge that would haunt many of the Mughal kings, was perhaps the reason for his erroneous judgements. Humayun was not someone who appreciated alcohol or being drunk but was definitely addicted to opium mixed with rose water. He even used opiates to torture his enemies, oftentimes getting them drunk or drugged. There is an instance when after winning the state of Champaner in Gujarat, he heard that the king Bahadur Shah had hidden away his treasure. Instead of torturing him, Humayun ordered his soldiers to keep the Shah drunk until he gave up the place where he had hidden his treasures.

Soon forced to wage war on three fronts, he was defeated and expelled from India by the formidable Sher Shah Suri. He fled to Persia, where he spent the next dozen years trying to persuade the temperamental and very eccentric Safavid ruler Shah Tahmasp to help him regain his territory. It took Humayun 15 years to win back his empire in India. Humayun's return changed the cultural and social landscape of India permanently. He returned to India accompanied by a large retinue of Persian noblemen, artisans, poets, courtesans and linguists, and signalled an important change in Mughal court culture. It brought in refinement and a finely developed sense of aesthetics hitherto unseen. Unfortunately, he soon died when he fell down the stairs of his library in Delhi, leaving behind a very young son.

Only just turned 13, Akbar inherited the lands won by his grandfather. Though young and uneducated, his intense curiosity, innate wisdom and concern for the people in his domain turned Babur's foothold in India into the mighty Mughal Empire. To control and unify the vast Mughal state, Akbar established a centralized system of administration and adopted a policy of conciliation among the conquered rulers through diplomacy and marriage. It is reported that no less than 5,000 women lived in Akbar's palace, of whom chroniclers hasten to reassure 'only' about 300 were his wives or concubines.

Ruling over a religiously and culturally diverse empire, he steered clear of a mere Islamic identity, including people from all other religions and walks of life in his court. He established a library at Fatehpur Sikri exclusively for women and mandated education for both Muslims and Hindus throughout the realm. Akbar's courts at Delhi, Agra and Fatehpur Sikri became great centres of the arts, letters and learning. Finally, Timurid and Persio-Islamic culture began to merge and blend with indigenous Indian elements, creating a unique Indo-Persian culture evident in the arts, painting and architecture.

These same Persian traditions also encouraged drinking, citing that wine is the best restorative for health, as much as other beneficial drugs, even an elixir.

When young, Akbar is said to have been an aficionado of arrack, a very heady palm wine, as well as *post*, a concoction made of diluted opium mixed with spices. In the *Akbarnama* (The Book of Akbar), the official chronicle of his reign, he admits to drinking some 18 cups of alcohol a day. Jahangir, too, in his memoir, talks about his father's drinking habits and remembers an incident where Akbar, having consumed too many cups of wine, couldn't mount an elephant. Rodolfo Acquaviva, a Jesuit missionary, too recalls that Akbar 'went to such excesses in drinking that the merit of fasting was lost in the demerit of inebriation'.[20]

Sir Thomas Roe, among the first ambassadors of England to the Mughal courts, reported that 'the smell of wine emitted from Akbar's court'.[21] All his senior noblemen drank wine with him, especially on special occasions and hunting trips. Father Monserrate, a Jesuit missionary who visited Akbar's court, noted on the other hand that the emperor was more partial to opium than alcohol, and though Akbar enforced a no-drinking rule in court, he allowed foreign visitors to consume their tipple.

In the *Akbarnama* he narrates an incident where he is injured in a fight. Akbar had nine men of exceptional calibre in his court, who have come to be known as the Navaratnas or 'nine gems'. Man Singh, one of the Navaratnas and the commander-in-chief of Akbar's army, was once at a drinking party where, after many hours of drinking, the conversation turned to the bravery of Rajput men. A completely inebriated Akbar, to prove that he was braver than the Rajputs, wanted to impale himself with his sword. The shocked crowd however was too drunk to stop the emperor, until Man Singh pushed Akbar to the ground, wounding him even as the sword fell to the floor. Believing that Man Singh was attacking him, an angry Akbar beat up his Rajput commander who had only tried to save him. It took a while to clear up the misunderstanding.

In time, Akbar transformed and decided to regulate the use of alcohol both for himself as well as the general public. Drinking was widespread among the Muslim aristocracy, and the common people too were partial to it. Ironically, there was no penalty under the law for the sale of liquor. Realizing the impracticality of total prohibition, Akbar made a compromise by controlling the use of intoxicants. He passed a new legislation that regulated consumption while permitting moderate drinking. 'He opened several bars under administration supervision and a register was maintained to record the quantity of alcohol sold to every individual.'[22] He also allowed a liquor shop to be opened near the palace. He ordered public bars to be placed under official supervision, where prices were fixed and excessive drinking and disorderly behaviour were made punishable: in case a Muslim was found intoxicated and two witnesses presented evidence against him before a qazi, he received 80 lashes while a slave would receive 20 stripes.

But the twin plagues of alcohol and opium hovered over his family, with two of his three sons, Murad and Daniyal, both dying from chronic intemperance. When Murad as well as his nine-year-old son died, in an effort to save Daniyal, Akbar insisted that he take a vow of temperance like his great grandfather. Daniyal agreed and even took the oath and destroyed his drinking vessels like Babur. But soon, unable to curb the habit, he started drinking again. Akbar even appointed guardsmen to watch over Daniyal to ensure that he stayed clean, but all the father's efforts were in vain – shortly after, Daniyal died from drinking spurious liquor that was mixed with gunpowder residue.

Always a disturbed and tense relationship, the schism between the father and his only surviving son widened; desperate to keep the dynasty alive, Akbar's chief consort Salima personally travelled to Allahabad to bring about a rapprochement between Salim and Akbar. And, against his better judgement, a dying Akbar placed his imperial turban on the head of his eldest son. For almost half a century, Jalaluddin Muhammad Akbar was the master of the largest empire since Asoka. He is still hailed as the greatest of the Mughals, an empire-builder of genius and a brilliant administrator, for his religious syncretism and tolerance that he brought to polity.

---

'Alcohol and the Mughals,' wrote the historian Qaiser, 'went hand in hand.'[23] And nowhere was it more obvious than when Jahangir came to power. Completely addicted to wine and opium, driven by his own demons and insecurities, unable to fulfil his territorial ambitions and surrounded by court intrigue, an ambitious wife and violence all around him, much of Salim's life was lived out in an alcoholic haze. Salim naively begins his memoirs with, 'My father, whether in cups or in his sober moments, calls me Shaiku Baba,' and he was indeed a cherished child.[24] The eldest son of Akbar and his Rajput wife, he was a precious gift from God, born with the blessings of Sheikh Salim Chishti, a revered Sufi saint who lived in Sikri, and was named after him. Indulged and pampered, Salim had a slew of tutors who taught him Persian, Turkish, Arabic, Hindi, arithmetic, history and geography. Along with all this, he unfortunately also learnt to drink from a very early age.

Though the favoured child, Salim's relationship with his father Akbar was fraught with angst from the very beginning. Even if he lacked his father's abilities, Salim was not without military ambitions, dreaming of conquering territory across the river Oxus, the lands of his Timurid ancestors. More importantly, he wanted to inherit the throne which, despite him being the heir apparent, was not assured, making him insecure and leading to direct confrontations with his father. In 1598, for example, Akbar saw an opportunity to invade Turan, a kingdom in Central Asia he had long set his eyes on, and decided to send Salim to lead the expedition. Salim refused.

Thirty years old with embarrassingly little conquest to his credit and already an alcoholic, Salim's refusal not just angered his father but also earned him the ire of Abu'l Fazl, Akbar's most trusted confidant and courtier: 'That pleasure-loving youth,' he wrote, 'could not wean himself off alcohol.'[25] Believing that the doggedly loyal

Fazl wielded too much influence on his father, Salim turned against him, considering him to be the greatest threat to his chances of succeeding Akbar. Nor was Fazl the only one. Akbar was inordinately fond of his grandchildren, so much so that it led Fazl to write: 'The affectionate sovereign loved his grandchildren more than his sons.'[26]

To compound the problem, there was the ongoing struggle with his own eldest son, Khusrau, whom Akbar was inclined to name his successor. Inevitably, in the years prior to Akbar's death, his court became a political cauldron, a snake-pit of intrigue between the rival camps of Salim and Khusrau. Impatient to inherit the throne as well as get his father out of the way, Khusrau rebelled but was defeated by the imperial forces near Jalandhar where he was caught and blinded by Salim. He also then turned on the Sikh guru Arjan, who had assisted the rebellious Khusrau with money and men, and had him tortured to death. The story gets murkier with Salim getting Abu'l Fazl murdered too.

Salim was 36 when he finally ascended the throne, assuming the name of Nur-ud-Din Muhammad Jahangir. An amiable man, oftentimes playful and gentle, despite by his own admission having had several people killed, he did not possess the vision, idealism and genius of Akbar. However, he wisely chose to leave the administrative machinery of his father intact. He also followed his father's ideals of liberalism and secularism, letting the empire flourish on its own. Among these worthy orders – abolishing certain taxes and punishments, building wells and hospitals – was one that banned the manufacture and sale of alcohol! More than his administrative abilities (or the lack thereof), Jahangir is known for his love of the arts, painters and poets, and his own biography, the *Jahangirnama*.

He writes with astonishing candour about how he instantly fell in love with wine when he first tasted it. Parvati Sharma, in her book on Jahangir, says, '"Liked" is not the word for it: in nine years, by his own meticulous measure, Salim had progressed from two gulps of sweet wine to "twenty phials of double-distilled spirits, fourteen during the day and rest at night." To clarify, he goes on, that is "six Hindustani seers, which is equivalent to one-and-a-half Iranian maunds".'[27]

Inexplicably, through his alcoholic haze, Jahangir soon realized that his youth had been misspent and if he continued in the same vein, the throne that he had fought so hard for would soon be lost to death. He tells the story himself: 'After nine years of untrammelled drinking, things got so bad that my hands shook and trembled so badly I couldn't drink myself but had to have others help me.'[28] It is a miracle that he saw the imminent danger of the consequences of his binges. Salim consulted his Hakim Humam, who told him 'with no beating around the bush, "Highness, the way you're drinking, in another six months – God forbid – things will be so bad it will be beyond remedy."'[29]

The dormant Timurid genes miraculously kicked in; displaying a hitherto unexploited strength of will, Jahangir slowly and methodically started to drink less. 'He substituted some of the alcohol with philonium (an all-spice drug of opium, saffron, spikenard, honey, etc.); diluted his spirits with grape wine ("two parts wine to one part spirits"); he drank only in the evenings (except the eve of Friday, a sacred day); and over the course of seven years, he went from twenty cups of double-distilled liquor to six cups of fortified wine supplement with two and a half grams of opium.'[30] He jots in verse:

> We cast the heart's core into the limpid tears.
> The wine was without effect; we threw opium into it.[31]

In the midst of all the court intrigue and addiction, Jahangir found the time to marry several times and also accumulate numerous concubines. He was almost 40 when he set his eyes on what would become yet another extreme addiction. He first saw Mehr-un-Nissa at the palace *meena bazaar* during Nowruz, the Parsi new year. Beautiful, witty and volatile with crackling intelligence and ambition, at 34, she was no nubile virgin. Born into a family of Persian nobility, Mehr-un-Nissa was 17 when she was married by royal consent to Ali Quli Khan Istalju, a Persian immigrant.

Jahangir was immediately smitten and wanted her in his harem – an offer she shrewdly spurned, professing to be faithful to her husband. Here the narratives vary. According to some accounts she was already a widow when she met Jahangir, while according to other stories, he had Sher Afghan Khan conveniently murdered under trumped-up charges of sedition and conspiracy to rebel. In any event, Mehr-un-Nissa became Salim's twentieth and last wife, and the title of Nur Jahan (light of the world) was conferred on her to match his Nur-ud-Din Jahangir.

A besotted Jahangir continued to revel in his daily, albeit reduced, consumption of alcohol and opium. The shrewd Nur Jahan, seeing the wasted state of her husband and his entire family as well as their disinterest in matters of state, stepped in, slowly winning her husband's trust; soon she became the most powerful woman in the Mughal Empire, then at the peak of its power and glory. In Jahangir's own words: 'I have sold my kingdom to my beloved queen for a cup of wine and a dish of soup.' Although she produced no heirs, she became the real power behind the throne, attending court and sitting discreetly beside Jahangir behind a *jharokha* (trellised window).

Jahangir initially consulted her on matters of governance but slowly let her make her own decisions. Intelligent and a quick decision maker, she was handed over the charge of the imperial seal and administered the distribution of jagirs (land parcels), with her consent needed for every document or order. She became the only Mughal empress to have coinage struck in her name and was even decreed a *nishan*, a privilege reserved for royal males. As Jahangir's dependence on alcohol and opium grew, so did his reliance on his empress, who appointed her father and then her brother as prime ministers.

In an empire that had been built on the foundation of the marauding Mongols, non-violence and military inaction could be seen as a major defect. And although Jahangir sent his son on several military campaigns, his rule is not remembered for its military conquests, but as a landmark of stability. Despite his addictions, Jahangir was an aesthete – as was his wife – and so, assured of their patronage, artisans and painters, poets and philosophers thronged to the Mughal court.

The Europeans arrived too, vying for trade and wealth. Spices, muslin, broadcloth, gems, indigo and opium had by then been traded for over a thousand years, as had alcohol. During the reigns of Babur and Jahangir, the quantities imported, especially of wines, saw a multifold increase. Records and journals written by foreign travellers as well as members of the Mughal court indicate the excessive use of alcohol at both the court and among commoners. Alcohol was also considered a gift of goodwill, especially among merchants, who used it as part of their negotiations, thereby becoming an important part of the trading process.

Thomas Roe, the English ambassador who had first arrived at Jahangir's court, continued to be a regular presence there as well as his favourite drinking companion for over three years; he gives an elaborate testimony of the emperor's fondness for drinks. In 1616, Jahangir celebrated his birthday at Ajmer and sent for Thomas Roe, who was given a rousing welcome and offered wine in a golden cup. The wine was so strong that after a sip, Roe started sneezing, which is said to have greatly amused the emperor.

While there are innumerable Mughal miniature paintings and buildings that bear testimony to the brilliance of Mughal aesthetics, some of the most enduring images of Jahangir are his portraits of him holding a cup. And these cups in themselves became an impressive expression of Mughal art and their drinking tradition. Drinking cups especially made for the emperor were crafted from different materials, showcasing the development of fine arts. The wine cup became Jahangir's official emblem; he even had commemorative coins minted that have come to be known as the 'Bacchanalian coins', in which he is depicted holding a wine cup in his right hand with a halo around his head. Embedded with precious stones, these cups were made of copper, silver, gold and green jade, and often had couplets about wine engraved on them.

As pomp and splendour grew in Jahangir's court, intrigue too intensified. The emperor's third son Khurram, whose mother was a Rajput princess, was the main contender to the Mughal throne, though his stepmother Nur Jahan who had no children of her own had plans for her brother. She managed to send Khurram away on a military expedition to the Deccan, where the prince, hearing of his father's failing health, first killed his popular brother Khusrau. He led a rather futile rebellion against his father and his stepmother, only to be defeated and exiled for three years. However, unable to stand the anxieties bought on by the intrigue and palace machinations, Jahangir fled to Kashmir, a place he called his own paradise, where he died in 1627. Khurram immediately rushed to Agra, claimed the throne, deposed Nur Jahan and exiled her to Lahore.

Jahangir is often seen as a fickle, alcoholic and opium-addicted emperor, though his reign saw a long period of peace, prosperity and stability, giving India a heightened sense of aesthetics and culture that prevails even today. As for Jahangir, all he ever wanted, as he himself says, was 'a bottle of wine and a piece of meat to keep myself merry'.[32]

The battle for the throne was a continuous saga in Mughal history as they had no laws of succession, the 'strength of the sword' and the ruthlessness with which it was wielded being the only measure. The travails of Khurram, who ascended the throne as Shah Jahan, had only just begun. Though he had exiled Nur Jahan, being politically astute, she had her daughter Ladli Begum (from her first husband) married to Shahryar, another son of Jahangir, and manipulated to get him to overthrow Shah Jahan.

Ironically, the man who would become famous all over the world for his love story immortalized in stone ascended the throne with a lot of blood on his hands. He murdered his brother Shahryar; his nephews Dawar and Garshasp, sons of his other brother Khusrau whom he had had killed earlier; as well as his cousins Tahmuras and Hoshang, sons of the late Prince Daniyal Mirza, who had died an alcoholic.

Shah Jahan had grown up witnessing his father's addictions. He had also lost two of his uncles and brother Parvez to alcohol, all of which created a lifelong aversion to alcohol. Jahangir writes about how hard he had to try to get Shah Jahan to have a few sips of wine on his twenty-fourth birthday. It was also forced upon him by his father's courtiers, who cited doctors as claiming that wine was beneficial in moderation. To support the point, one of them also quoted a verse by the Persian physician Avicenna:

> Wine is a raging enemy, a prudent friend;
> A little is an antidote, but much is snake's poison.
> In much there is no little injury,
> In a little there is much profit.[33]

Despite this active persuasion, Shah Jahan avoided drinking for personal rather than religious reasons and remained a reluctant drinker throughout his life. Though he did not drink regularly, he never imposed prohibition on others, and in fact, due to his leniency, the consumption of alcohol increased during his reign.

Niccolao Manucci, an Italian traveller who came to Surat in 1638, attests to the fact that the emperor was not a drinker, but he did nothing to remedy the growing problem. On the other hand, the English East India Company (EIC) records reveal that the emperor was fond of drinks; the English merchant William Fremlen wrote to the company in London that he had been requested to procure grape wine as well as two large cases of Allegent and Canary wines.[34] If Shah Jahan drank at all, he too, like Babur, eventually gave it up completely, had the entire stock of the court's wine thrown into the Chambal River and the wine utensils of gold broken and distributed among the poor.

When he was 15, Shah Jahan met the 14-year-old Arjumand Banu at one of the booths in the royal bazaar and immediately fell in love. He already had two other wives. Unusual for the time, they waited five years to get married; Arjumand became his favourite wife and as Mumtaz Mahal bore him 14 children, dying at 38 in childbirth. Shah Jahan is renowned for the many architectural wonders that he had built, including the Red Fort and Jama Masjid in Delhi and the fort and Moti Masjid in Agra, but he is best remembered for the magnificent marble mausoleum the Taj Mahal, which has remained an endearing ode to his beloved wife. He however soon fell ill, and the belief that he would not recover once again triggered the battle for succession.

Shah Jahan had designated his eldest son Dara Shikoh as the crown prince, who was deposed and murdered by his brother Aurangzeb. After being stabbed to death, Dara Shikoh's head was removed and, according to a report, sent to his father. Aurangzeb also pressured two of Dara Shikoh's wives to accept his hand in marriage. While all this was going on, the luckless Shah Jahan recovered from his illness, only to be immediately imprisoned at the Agra Fort, where he lived for eight long years, eventually dying broken-hearted looking at the Taj.

Aurangzeb's accession to the throne heralded the decline of the mighty Mughal Empire. All the kings up until Aurangzeb had certainly been flamboyant and cosmopolitan but benevolent, largely secular rulers who were concerned about the welfare of their kingdom. Though Muslim, they allowed religious freedom, stayed away from religious dogma and married Indian princesses whether out of love or convenience; many of the kings who ascended the throne were children by Rajput women.

These highly tolerant and sophisticated regimes now made way for an intolerant one. Shunning the liberal humanitarianism of his ancestors, their secularism and convenient interpretation of Islam, Aurangzeb made a volte-face towards Sunni orthodoxy, which was completely at odds with his Central Asian Hanafi ancestry. Deeming all non-Muslims to be infidels, he embraced stringent religious canons, ushering in an era that transformed the cultural and theological landscape of India. A bigoted, ruthless and cruel ruler who restricted personal freedoms and imposed strict religious tenets, his goal was to bring true Islamic governance to all the lands under the Mughal Empire. Under the new laws of his regime, in an attempt to end socially corrupt practices, he abolished gambling, prostitution, bars, taverns as well as the sale of alcohol.

The story goes that while he was still a young prince in the Deccan, he fell in love with a dancing girl with whom he often drank wine. The girl died under unfortunate circumstances and following her death Aurangzeb vowed never to drink again, even thanking

God for taking the girl's life as it stopped him from drinking. Strictly opposed to any form of intoxication, he attempted to prohibit drug and alcohol consumption within the empire. He ordered the chief muhtasib (the supervisor of bazaars and trade) along with a large body of subordinates to explain the ill-effects of the use of intoxicants. Religious police forces were appointed to ensure that people didn't dance, sing or drink; the only exception was for Christians, who were allowed to produce alcohol in limited quantities.

Alas, he met with little success. Aurangazeb's effort to impose prohibition within his empire was one of the more spectacular policy failures of his reign. Niccolao Manucci, a Venetian doctor and traveller who lived and died in India, provides one of the few first-hand European accounts of the courts of Shah Jahan and Aurangzeb. In his *Storia do Mogor*, he writes that every person in the kingdom, with the exception of Aurangzeb himself, was addicted to alcohol. The Mughal drinking culture still firmly remained focused on wine, but in contrast to the open exuberance of the previous kings, drinking went behind closed doors, inside private homes and chambers. And, ironically, rather than being a deterrent, private drinking led to overindulgence once removed from public scrutiny and the censorious eyes of the emperor. He could not even put his own house in order; when he heard that his son Shah Alam (Bahadur Shah I) had started drinking while in Kabul, he immediately told him to return to Delhi but did little to deter the young man from getting imported wines from Europe and Persia delivered to him secretly.

Sons apart, Aurangzeb's sisters Jahanara and Roshanara too were fond of their tipple. Both were feisty women, and Jahanara especially was not one to meekly follow the diktats of her brother. Well known for her interest in Sufism and a respected author of her time, her biography of the Sufi saint Salim Chishti, *The Confidant of Spirits*, is highly regarded for its literary quality. When Shah Jahan moved his capital to Delhi, Jahanara was responsible for five of the nineteen imperial buildings built in the city and also laid out the iconic central avenue of Chandni Chowk with its bazaars. As the Padshah Begum, Jahanara was responsible for trade with the English and the Dutch, even having her own ship called the *Sahibi*.

A wealthy woman in her own right, she also struggled with an alcohol problem. Besides literature and the arts, she enjoyed the finer things in life and drank her own blend of wine mixed with rose water.

Legend has it that when Jahanara came to know that the mullahs were going to extend prohibition to include women, she invited the wives of all the mullahs to a wine party. When Aurangzeb came to break the news to Jahanara, pointing to the intoxicated wives of the mullahs she said that the mullahs should first set their own houses in order.

By Aurangzeb's reign the empire, which had been the world's largest economy, accounting for over 25 per cent of the global GDP at the time, began to decline. He ruled with an iron fist for 49 years, and after his death, a war of succession once again began among his three surviving sons: Muazzam, the governor of Kabul; Azam, the governor of Gujarat; and Kam Bakhsh, the governor of the Deccan. Muazzam emerged victorious and ascended the Mughal throne with the title of Bahadur Shah I. Poor administrative abilities, alcoholism, mismanagement and infighting soon saw the Mughal Empire sink into chaos and violent feuds, with four emperors successively ascending the throne in just one year.

There began a steady decline in the authority of the Mughal emperor, and the people who had served under these emperors started flexing their muscles and exercising their individual political identities. These breakaway factions formed new dynasties and held command over important provinces like Hyderabad and Awadh. Although they continued to recognize and respect the Mughal emperor in Delhi, by the eighteenth century, the Mughal Empire witnessed complete fragmentation.

Fourteen kings ruled or tried to rule after Aurangzeb's death, ending with Emperor Bahadur Shah Zafar, who was coronated in 1837. By this time, the empire that had once held sway over much of the Indian subcontinent had completely disintegrated. The twentieth king Zafar was merely a titular head, as the Mughal Empire was now restricted to the walled city of Old Delhi. The British, though in complete control, felt uneasy that Zafar as a Mughal emperor would become a rallying point for a rebellion and held him prisoner, restricting him to his living quarters in the Red Fort. Lorded over by the British, Bahadur Shah Zafar was acutely aware of his diminished circumstances and fall from glory. However broken and ill, the proclivity to drink persisted, and he devoted all his time to his two favourite activities, drinking and writing poetry. Eventually exiled to Rangoon after the Revolt of 1857, shorn of all luxuries and liquor, the last Mughal emperor, with a mere handful of relatives, breathed his last in a shabby wooden house and was consigned to an unmarked grave.

But what a legacy the Mughals left behind! Centuries of strife, mayhem and hedonism were interspersed with the golden age of Indian architecture, painting and literature, all attributed to the evolved sense of aesthetics that was a part of the Timurid legacy.

Babur was curious, literate and articulate, setting the trend for each of the kings who followed him to write their own autobiographies. All of these without exception are candid accounts of their lives, harems and observations, and reflect their interest in a variety of subjects ranging from statecraft, military expedition, weapons, nature, the environment, poetry, music, paintings, architecture and their favourite pastime, wine parties. So, it comes as no surprise that in many of the literary works spanning the 350 years of Mughal rule – poetry and verse, ghazals and shayari – there are innumerable references to alcohol and the experience of intoxication.

This was particularly true of Sufi literature. A school of Islamic mysticism, Sufism had been in India from the time of the Delhi Sultanate but came to the fore during Mughal rule. The Mughal kings were devotees of different Sufi orders and promoted both Sufism and

Sufi literature. All the kings, much like their Turkish and other Central Asian ancestors, revered Sufi holy men who sought direct experience of the divine.

Given the ubiquitous use of alcohol and intoxicants among the members of the court and commoners, and much like the Hindu Brahmins before them believing that the use of intoxicants altered minds and was a path to seek the divine, Sufi literature is suffused with the use of wine and drinking cups as symbols.

These mystical poets liberally used the metaphors of 'wine', 'cup', 'tavern' and 'wine-bearer' to help perceive the phenomenon of a spiritual world. Khamriyat was a special genre of Sufi poetry that focused on wine but needed a complex Sufi lexicon for the interpretation of these verses, lest the oft-used metaphors be misunderstood or misinterpreted by the uninitiate.

The Sufis themselves followed in the footsteps of Umar Ibn al-Farid, the legendary twelfth-century Arab poet who is held in the highest esteem as the greatest of mystic poets. His two masterpieces – 'The Wine Ode', a beautiful rendition on the 'wine' of divine bliss, and 'the Poem of the Sufi Way' – are considered by many to be the pinnacle of mystical verse and are reverently memorized by Sufis and devout Muslims even today.

The ecstasy described by Sufis is a condition a person reaches through inner transformation, the rapture that one gets from a profound spiritual experience – one that lead to an experience of 'divine intoxication'.

Wine that is forbidden for the sober,
Is allowed for the drunk dervish.
O, cupbearer, don't tell it's enough for me —
I will drink till I wine ends! (Rumi, *Rubaiyat*, 1108)[35]

Whether in the form of poetry, literature, art or the Taj Mahal, the Mughals have left an indelible stamp on India, a monumental legacy that has permeated and enriched every aspect of Indian life.

Their empire crumbled under the weight of their own excesses and hedonism, and the advent of colonialism, but the Mughals never truly left. Their sophisticated presence is woven into our lives and lives on in the verses of the ghazals, the language we speak, the clothes we wear and even in the many dishes we continue to relish.

# 5

# Colonial Capers: Spirits of Empire

As seafaring nations rose in the west, adventurers lured by tales of roads paved with gold set sail in an attempt to conquer the unknown world. The Mughals permitted trade with the French, the Danes, the Portuguese and the English, who, while carving out territories for themselves, brought with them – besides gunpower – their own food and drink, as markers of their identity.

By the eighteenth century, alcohol had become the second-largest revenue earner for the EIC, which had set up excise systems, licensing taverns, taxing indigenous drinks and regulating distilleries.

The prohibitive prices of importing liquor and the long wait for it resulted in these foreigners brewing liquor using local ingredients. Soon, India was awash with locally brewed and distilled beer, gin and tonic, whisky and Scotch.

If many of the narratives about Indian mythologies, religious beliefs, social habits, politics and the histography of invading adventurers are closely entwined with liquor, the story of the alcohol that came in with the early foreigners far exceeds them all. India, along with Mesopotamia, China and Egypt, was home to one of the oldest civilizations, which led to continuous cultural development within a specific geographical location. As celebrated as the other three for its urban development, education, spiritual mastery, wealth and natural resources, it's a small wonder that India attracted the attention of foreigners, mainly to plunder, but also to learn, assimilate and understand its little-known culture. Two of the earliest and better known of these conquerors were our neighbours, the Persians Darius and Xerxes, who crossed the Oxus and Indus to occupy large parts of the Punjab. Herodotus, the Greek historian, mentions that the lands they conquered (present-day Sindh and parts of Punjab) became the twentieth satrapy of the Achaemenid Empire as well as its richest, providing 360 talents of gold dust, the highest of any province.

They were soon followed by the Greeks and Macedonians, and one man in particular: Alexander the Great.

Alexander was undoubtedly of the world's greatest military leaders, establishing one of the largest empires in history, extending from Greece to northwestern India, by the time he was 30. He marched into India in 326 BCE towards Taxila, where he encountered the army of King Porus, the sovereign of the kingdom between the rivers Chenab and Jhelum. History celebrates Alexander as a conquering hero, but disturbing stories of moral turpitude persist, and historians agree that his fundamental problem was with alcohol.

Alexander spent most of his downtime listening to sycophants while guzzling wine, reportedly dying during a drinking orgy in Babylon. Legend has it that to honour the death of his trusted advisor Calanus, he organized a handful of 'funeral games', one of which was an epic drinking contest, where 35 of the 42 brave souls who accepted the challenge died on the spot. The winner was apparently a Greek soldier who drank nearly four gallons of wine and lived to tell the tale for a couple of days before also dying of alcohol poisoning.

Although Alexander's encounter with India was brief, the impact of that encounter was enormous and lasting. One of the strangest and most striking products of that legacy emerged several hundred years later in the form of ancient Greek literature's last and longest epic poem: the *Dionysiaca*. Written by Nonnus of Panopolis, the epic weaves dozens of myths around a central theme: the conquest of India.

Experts know almost nothing about Nonnus's life but date the *Dionysiaca* as being written sometime around the fourth century CE. The India-conquering hero of Nonnus's great poem was not Alexander but Dionysus, the Greek god of wine. Legends have long connected Dionysus with Asia, as he was supposed to have arrived in Greece from the East on a chariot pulled by exotic panthers, teaching the art of wine-making to various Asian cultures along the way. Nonnus transformed these stories, adding every available myth, thereby creating a poem of unprecedented length and scope.

The *Dionysiaca* begins with Zeus, king of the Greek gods, ordering Dionysus to travel to India, whose inhabitants refuse to worship him. The Indians stubbornly prefer their own ancestral gods of fire and water. Worse, they refuse to drink wine,

Dionysus's 'care-forgetting vintage'. Dionysus gathers an enormous army that marches across the ancient world to India, collecting a slew of lovers along the way. His foe is Deriades, ruler of India and son of the river Jhelum. Deriades, being half river himself, drinks only water and scorns Dionysus's beverage. Helped by Brahmins well versed in sorcery, Deriades fights several battles with Dionysus before he and the entire land finally succumb to the god's influence and the power of alcohol.[1]

So, like so much else, we can also blame our drinking habits on a foreign hand.

Interaction with the Greeks, however, did not die with Alexander. The Greeks appointed Megasthenes, famed for his book *Indica* about his time in the country, as ambassador to the court of Chandragupta Maurya; he was followed by Deimachus, who was sent to Chandragupta's son Bindusara's court. The Greeks were followed by the Chinese, who came in search of the Buddha and Nirvana. Prominent among the hundreds of Chinese monks who came to India were Faxian, Xuanzang and Yijing, whose detailed accounts of their journeys provided a glimpse into India, its rulers, social customs and behaviour.

For some, India was a sacred and mystical, even utopian realm. Others saw India as a land inhabited by civilized and sophisticated people, while others still saw Indians as barbaric and uncultured, steeped in superstition and in need of education and 'modernization'. So they came – invaders, travellers, itinerant traders, missionaries, artisans, adventurers – men who sought to experience, see and partake of India, intrigued by its wealth, customs, faiths, rich culture and other exotic offerings.

The age of adventure was pioneered by the seafaring Europeans who sought to discover new lands and fortunes for themselves and their regents. Tales of the riches of India had been circulating for centuries, which inspired many to find sea routes rather than undertaking the very arduous overland expeditions. First came the Portuguese followed by the Danes, French and English in search of fame, fortune and, initially, spice. Appearing as traders and missionaries, they came bearing exotic gifts for the local kings and Christianity for the poor.

Soon, colonies managed by governors-general were established, factories set up for manufacturing and warehouses for trade, with soldiers to manage them all. The story of the European colonists in India is one that is awash with alcohol. Unaccustomed to the heat, dust, malaria and mosquitoes, they soon grew nostalgic for their homeland, especially their climate, women and booze. Unable to communicate with the locals, rendered lethargic by the incessant heat and surrounded by sycophantic servants, all they had to keep them company was alcohol. Drinking was a common enough practice among the 'natives' so there was plenty of liquor available, albeit all local brews. Nostalgia for their usual tipple led to imports, with each nationality bringing in what they were used to back home.

Wine had long ago found its way to the east coast of India in Greek amphoras with the early traders, finding favour with the locals, who were soon disappointed to learn that grapes could not be grown along the Malabar coastline. Moreover, wine did not keep well, turning rancid in the heat and humidity. Soon enough, an alternate surfaced; *madeira*, a strong, sweet wine produced in the volcanic island by the same name in Portugal, began to be imported to India. Madeira proved to be the wine maverick, actually benefiting from the intense weather in the subcontinent, with gin and whisky being rare imports. 'Gentlemen always took special care to be supplied with the best French wines and the oldest Madeira that could be purchased.'[2] The added advantage was that women too could drink wines like madeira while they weren't permitted other spirits.

Naturally, trading in madeira took off in a big way. What started off as an import of 100 pipes of liquor ended up becoming 6,400 pipes by the end of the seventeenth century, accounting for 40 per cent of all liquor sales in Madras (now Chennai). Back in Portugal, even conservative traders were 'forced to accept Indian contracts and develop bases in that part of the world or face bankruptcy'.[3] But madeira was not the only thing the Portuguese introduced to India. Many of the staples that are taken for granted today, like potatoes, tomatoes, chillies, pineapples and the cashew nut, were bought to India by the Portuguese. Cashew, which is native to Brazil, was introduced to India as early as 1514. The cashew apple, which is not commonly consumed due to its astringent taste, proved to be an excellent source for distillation and was easily transformed into a unique and potent local Goan brew called *feni*, whose very name has Indian roots. It is believed to be derived from the Sanskrit word *phena*, which means 'froth', thanks to the bubbles that form a light froth when feni is poured into a glass.

Blessed with a long shelf life and now labelled as a 'heritage drink', feni today is made from both coconut and cashew nut fruits, used as a base for many a cocktail and a favourite drink of the local Goans.

The Portuguese had gotten a head start in the lucrative business of exporting calico cloth and indigo from India, but the Dutch were not far behind, trading a lot more in spices than cotton along the Malabar Coast. And close on the heels of the Portuguese and the Dutch were the British. While the Jesuit missions at the Mughal court assumed the character and function of an embassy and of neutrality, the intention was to further the interests of the Portuguese, whose power was already on the decline.

The watchful British were close at hand to seize the opportunity.

When Queen Elizabeth I signed a charter for a new trading mandate named the East India Company on New Year's Eve in 1600, little could she have imagined that the Company would become the driving force behind British economic development for over 250 years. The company's revenues would far exceed those of the Crown and its achievements would become the mainstay of British history; were it not for the machinations of the EIC, there would have been no empire, nor the resultant Commonwealth.

The treaty obtained in 1618 from the Mughal emperor Jahangir opened the ports of India to trade, and by the end of the century, the EIC's influence had spread throughout most of India, and the foundation was laid for the British empire.

Trade flourished, as did personal fortunes; the Mughal kings, inundated with expensive gifts from Europe, gave away more and more trade sanctions. Factories were set up at Surat and Bombay (now Mumbai), as were the British conclaves Fort St George and Fort William, bringing in more and more adventurous Englishmen into India.

Alcohol was inherently linked to the EIC, which brought in as well as traded in various alcoholic beverages, such as claret, port and madeira. The officers of EIC were notorious for their capacity to drink, frequently arousing the wrath of the Court of Directors back in London. As demand and consumption rose, brewers in Britain started to make ales especially suited to the rigours of the voyage and the heat of the colonies, giving birth to the 'India pale ale'.

And then there was gin.

Back in Europe, the Netherlands was struggling for independence from Spain, where English soldiers were sent to assist the Dutch revolt. This is apparently where they first got their taste for a drink made from the Juniper berry that the troops drank before going into battle, for 'Dutch courage'. This Dutch–English collaboration produced an enduring drink, called 'gin' for short – 40 per cent alcohol primarily flavoured with Juniper berries as well as a variety of herbs and spices. The gin craze spread like wildfire in Britain, so much so that the Parliament had to pass a law imposing a tax on the drink, which ended in riots.

The other half of Britain that wasn't drunk on gin was busy setting up the empire halfway across the world. The sudden influx of a large number of Britons who migrated to India obviously brought their favourite tipple gin with them as well. The struggling EIC had a number of their staff, soldiers in particular, getting infected with malaria and dying. So, the rather serendipitous 'discovery' of the cinchona tree bark and its active ingredient, quinine, as a treatment and preventive measure for malaria, led Britian to ship quinine powder in massive quantities to its Indian colonies. The concoction, though, was so bitter that most people were loath to take it. That is until the British soldiers started adding lime, sugar and water to the quinine, giving birth to Indian tonic water. Winston Churchill is supposed to have said, 'Gin &

Tonic has saved more English lives and souls than all the doctors in the Empire.' Whether he actually said it or not is moot, but gin and tonic was and remains a legacy of the Raj.

Apart from gin, quinine too played a huge role in Britain's global dominance. By manufacturing tonic water and supplying it to their colonies prone to malarial fever and other ailments, they ensured that their administration of the colonies stayed intact and healthy. In her widely acclaimed and highly detailed book *Science and Colonial Expansion: The Role of the British Royal Botanic Gardens*, author Lucile Brockway contends that the control of cinchona – and thus quinine – was key to the expansion of Britain in Asia and Africa. Gin and tonic soon enough became a staple among soldiers and gentry alike, especially in the exclusive British gymkhana clubs that remains a rather romantic reminder of the Empire.[4]

Detailed narratives, travelogues, diaries and long letters written home record the daily lives of the British in India. Some saw their stay in India, a place of heat, dust and diarrhoea, as banishment; others saw it as a privilege. A life of luxury came relatively cheap in India where even private soldiers, schoolteachers, the clergy and others who were poorly paid were able to pay natives for services and household work. So, even in the worst of circumstances it was an adventure – of sensory overdose.

Factory accounts record the magnitude of alcohol that was in circulation, ironically corroborating the tales of British excesses in Mughal chronicles. More often than not, arguments and concerns were over food and drink and the lack thereof. Widespread alcohol consumption was very much the norm; drinking habits in colonial India were not divided by gender, with women consuming drinks such as beer, port and sherry as often as men. Discussions about alcohol were de rigueur, a constant in all gatherings – rationing, the quality of liquor, local brews and new ingredients were all discussed and debated with great enthusiasm.

While initially much of the beer and wine was brought in from England, given the growing demand, locally brewed liquors started making their appearance. Taking their cue from the arrack that was distilled by the natives from palm and coconuts, the British started producing arrack for their own consumption that went into making punch, which was drunk in drams by all the Europeans in India. 'Punch' came from the Persian root *panj* or Hindi *panch*, meaning 'five', and was composed of five ingredients: arrack, sugar, lime juice, spices and water or tea.

At the beginning of the 1680s, physician Christoph Frike, who was born in Ulm and worked for the Dutch EIC, wrote: 'From the arac mentioned one also prepares various savoury massac and burabols, so soon resembling the cold bowls and lemons, by mixing the same with sugar, lemon-water and wine.'[5]

A similar recipe was sent by Peter Mundy who from 1628 to 1630 was a trader in Surat, where the British factories were located. He reports: 'Our strong drinke is Racke, like strong water, next a kinde of beere made of Course Sugar and other ingredients, pleasant to the taste and wholesome, but many tymes water. There is sometimes a Composition of Racke, water, sugar and Juice of Lymes called Chareboockhra.'[6] 'Racke' is arrack and 'course sugar' is jaggery, a traditionally unrefined cane sugar used throughout South and Southeast Asia. 'Chareboockhra' is a bastardized spelling of *char-bakhra*, also spelled *chaar bakhraa*, meaning 'four parts.'[7]

Punch was here to stay, though it has adopted a wide canvas these days, where you can throw in any leftover liquor and still make a delicious cocktail.

The British also started making some wines from grapes grown in the regions of Kashmir, Golconda and Baramati. Unfortunately, these vineyards were destroyed by American lice that travelled by ship to India and demolished entire fields of vine, bringing to an end the wine business in India, which is only just resurfacing.

Driven by a mix of personal ambition, greed, commercial interest, security concerns and the need for revenue, the EIC grew to be a dominant power when it secured the right to gather tax and customs duties in Bengal, India's richest province. By the mid-1850s, the EIC governed two-thirds of the subcontinent, with each of its three 'presidencies' – Bengal, Bombay and Madras – maintaining its own army. Given the potential deleterious effect of widespread drinking on manpower, social disorder and relations with Indians, the manner in which to monitor, regulate and restrict alcohol consumption became a cause for concern among the civil authorities and the military in particular.

If the problem of importing liquor was resolved by setting up local manufacturing and distilling units, there remained the more vexing problem of managing a rapidly growing army. Many a young man came from England in search of fame and fortune; at first, these had amounted to no more than a handful of factory guards, but they soon grew to a strength of 250,000.

A posting to the colonies, though seemingly adventurous, was not easy, fraught with complications and contradictions; military and civil duty in India typically lasted five-to-seven years, though for many it became permanent due to the high mortality rate. Given the arduous journey, the majority of civilians or soldiers who came to India on duty rarely returned to Britain. While a large part of the army was constituted by local recruits, the officers were largely foreigners who could not do without their daily tipple. In her book, *Vice in the Barracks: Medicine, the Military and the Making of Colonial India, 1780–1868*, Erica Wald asserts that the drinking habits of serving military men were largely divided into two groups dictated by rank and pay, with officers able to afford bottled beers and claret whilst lower-ranked soldiers drank mainly spirits such as arrack.[8]

Rationing was an integral part of army life. Records vary as to how much alcohol was issued in Madras, Bombay and Bengal. Though figures fluctuate, a standard issue of between one-third and two-thirds of a pint of raw spirits (that's two large drinks in today's world) per man per day was common, with the proviso that it be diluted with 'two waters' and consumed immediately.

William Russell recounts his travels as part of General Colin Campbell's campaign in his account, where he notes that beer was the preferred choice of beverage, writing: 'A bottle of beer! Why, it is nothing. I know men who take three at tiffin. I know men who declare they know men who take a dozen bottles of beer in the day and that they are the better for it.'[9] To counter a permanently drunk army, several policies were introduced – court martials, rationing where the supply of liquor was deliberately kept to a minimum, keeping the canteens dirty and shabby to discourage soldiers from using them – alas, to no avail. The problem persisted and there are numerous records of officers and men being indicted for drunkenness or overindulgence. Men found guilty of having been drunk on five separate occasions within a 12-month period were classed officially as habitual drunkards.

While the drunkenness and unruly behaviour of soldiers could be monitored through disciplinary action, court martials and suspensions, the civilian population was harder to control. Encouraged by the EIC to settle in India as part of the 'civilizing mission', men often found solace among native women. Alarmed at the rising consumption of liquor and the large number of European men who fell in love with women from the subcontinent, the fear was that civil European society would fall prey to anarchy and licentiousness.

Stories circulated that the local women whose job it was to make punch out of arrack would mix poison into the drink of those sailors who offended them in any way. Then there were the dangerous tales about inebriation and prostitution:

> In the cool of the evening you see them (public women) before the doors of their houses, which are for the most part small huts, and when the night comes, they place at the doors a candle or a lighted lamp for a signal. It is then, also that the shops where they sell tari are opened. It is brought from five or six coss distant in leather bottles, upon horses, which carry one on each side and go at a fast trot, and about 500 or 600 of them enter the town daily. The King derives from the tax which he places on this tari a very considerable revenue and it is principally on this account that they allow so many public women as they are the cause of the consumption of so much tari.[10]

So alcohol consumption, with its potential to bring about a decline in morals, was constantly under scrutiny. As in Britain, the issue of drinking was the subject of various measures related to curbing public disorder. According to Sam Goodman, historian Erica Wald asserts that the drinking habits of the serving men were divided into two groups and dictated by rank and pay who largely drank in public spaces. As she writes in *Vice in the Barracks*, 'The logic that drinking, especially Indian spirits, which were cheap and thus typically consumed by private soldiers, was the beginning of a slippery slope into gambling, vice, miscegenation, venereal disease, dishonour and eventual death, as stated in a memorandum by General O'Moore Creagh and Lord Kitchener, Commander in Chief of India in 1909.'[11]

Be that as it may, Kitchener's memo did little to disturb life in colonial India, which settled down into a lethargic routine, comprising retiring to the cooler hill stations during the summer months, intense political activity and long days of heat and idleness interspersed with regular drinking.

In sharp contrast to the idea that British rule in India brought about sobriety, discipline and civilized the 'natives', there have been a number of accounts documenting the heavy drinking, disorderly, illicit and often times criminal behaviour not just by the British but also all Europeans in India; there have been numerous contemporary accounts documenting the shenanigans and public misconduct especially of enlisted men. British regiments were known for extremely high alcohol consumption, often higher than even at home.

The British themselves were deeply worried about the extent of alcohol consumption. Temperance societies sprang up in Madras and Calcutta (now Kolkata), rationing was introduced and restrictions on arrack shops especially in cantonments.

> The drinking habits of our countrymen of all classes, are making a very injurious impression on the natives of India. Than the loafer, the vagrant, the drunken uneducated or debased European, whose passions are under no control, and who is amenable to no public opinion, nothing can be more sad to the Christian and more alarming to the statesman.[12]

As exemplified by the conduct – or misconduct – of Guy Athel Weston, a superintendent of police in the Punjab in 1919 who, after a modestly successful career of 18 years, was required to take compulsory retirement as a result of his continual difficulties with alcohol and inebriation. He was alleged to have committed 'a serious social indiscretion' involving alcohol, in which he appeared under the influence of liquor during a visit by Lieutenant Governor of the Punjab Sir Michael O'Dwyer to Gurugram, where Weston was then posted.

The Europeans, with their moral superiority, apparently did not quite behave as badly as the Englishmen, although in the early seventeenth century the Italian travel writer Manucci mentions that Europeans (or *firangi*s) were often derided by even the Mughals kings for their drunken behaviour, with Emperor Aurangzeb even issuing a diktat that they could not live within city limits.

The problem was not just about the white sahibs getting drunk, the constant worry was how this would impact the locals. This was coupled with the fear that such behaviour would instigate and encourage similar behaviour on the part of the native Indians themselves.

Then, of course, was the major domestic concern that the servants would empty the liquor cabinets of their masters, ending up drunk themselves. This was not without cause – there are again several stories about coach drivers, cooks and even mochis showing up drunk for work. An old 1907 postcard has an amusing drawing of an Indian servant certainly tipsy after drinking from his white master's bottle of whisky.

But, unconcerned by the alarm caused to the Company Board in London, young men continued to drink, take Indian mistresses and beget children with them. In *Indian Dust Devils* (1937), Harry Hobbs writes of his early days in Calcutta, whereupon he lodged as part of a 'chummery', a rented property shared by a group of unmarried men who split the costs of living. Hobbs writes that his chummery was characterized by drinking, either in the house or at a local hotel bar, and that the opinions and habits of the men he shared his lodgings with were 'crude – to say the least'.

Despite all the bad press and excesses, though, alcohol was not without its uses, at once being an agent of social interaction and an object of exchange, amicability and negotiation. It was perceived as being integral to the dynamics of pre-colonial India. Thomas Best and several officials of the EIC in the seventeenth century remarked that wine was not a commodity of trade in the subcontinent; rather, as Best advised his superiors at the EIC, it was 'best for presents fitt to be given in these countryes, that you send yearly 5 or 6 cases of bottles filled with hott waters (that is, spirits)'.[13] Alcohol in any form was used to placate and negotiate, bribe, gain access to the Mughal courts and get the necessary *farmans*. Tales of bribery and violence abound as a result of alcohol but are ironically also placated with it.

Despite all the angst that brewing, rationing, policing and keeping the army and population in check caused, the enormous revenue considerations and the fiscal policy of Britain led to the establishment of distilleries and liquor and opium shops in large numbers, leading to a steady increase in consumption, spreading misery and ruin among much of the working class of India.

The stated agenda was to counter the menace of increased alcohol consumption and the manufacture of illicit liquor by controlling and taxing the sale and manufacture of alcohol. The policy was completely successful in that there was an increase of revenue within a two-year period from £2,300,000 to £4,200,000. The increase in revenue was explained as being obtained from increased duties and decreased consumption and that 'drunkenness, in the English sense of the term, hardly exists in India'.

In direct contrast and refuting this, Keshub Chunder Sen, the great social reformer, and leader of the Brahmo Samaj in 1870 wrote in a public appeal:

> It is indeed harrowing and painful to contemplate the extent to which sensuality, profligacy, and brutal revels on the one hand, and irreligion, blasphemy, and practical atheism on the other, are making ravages among all classes as a consequence of the spread of drunkenness.... In short, the use of intoxicating liquor has done more than anything else to degrade the physical, moral, and social condition of my countrymen.[14]

Samuel Smith from Flintshire, who worked with the Abkari department of the EIC, elaborated on 30 April 1889 about the new liquor policy:

> The new liquor and the lower prices made it available to everyone ... domestic servants, day labourers, and women, drinking to an extent I never noticed before. My coachman has tumbled off his box drunk. If I want a mochee to mend the harness I have to arrange that he shall be sober the night before. I can speak from personal observation that there are more drunkards in and about this city than I ever observed before.[15]

Complaints like these poured in from all over India; petitions were presented by Indians and Europeans and, finally, in 1883–84, a commission of inquiry was appointed – to no effect. The Indian National Congress, which the British recognized as an important educated and representative body of some 1,200 members, then passed this resolution: 'Due to the fact that a serious increase in the consumption of intoxicants has taken place under the systems of Abkari and excise now prevailing in India, the Government be respectfully urged to adopt a more improved system to discourage insobriety.'

Samuel Smith further adds:

> Even to-day the mass of Indians are abstainers. The consumption of drink is confined to a few comparatively … But whereas ten years ago there were perhaps 10,000,000 of drinkers in India, we have now turned them into 20,000,000, and at the rate we are going on we shall, in time, turn the 20,000,000 into 40,000,000 and the 40,000,000, into 80,000,000 … A wasteful system of finance has brought the Government of India to lean more and more on immoral sources of revenue, and so we go on poisoning the natives of India with drink as we have poisoned the Chinese with opium.[16]

The effects of alcohol were evident everywhere. One writer who managed the tea gardens in the Northeast that brought in labour from different parts of India wrote:

> I regret to state the sad fact that drunkenness among garden coolies has spread to an alarming degree. Since the introduction of this odious system in 1883, the consumption of country spirits has, I am certain, increased sevenfold (possibly more). Sunday is, of course, the great day for drinking, and driving by I have come across coolies lying literally dead drunk at intervals in the road, covered with mud from head to foot, and have had to have them rolled on one side to clear the way for my trap. One of my best men got leave one day, bought six bottles of country spirits at a shop about four miles away, and, on his way home, fell across the railway line, smashing his bottles, and lying insensible until, luckily, picked up by another coolie. It is needless to say that the drinking leads to rioting and wife beating; eases, however, seldom come before the notice of the Government.[17]

Even locally brewed liquor like *mahua*, traditionally restricted to women in villages, saw the advent of rapacious foreigners, which led to revolts across the land. After two thousand years of brewing their own liquor, the locals were loath to pay taxes to the invading white men. According to an essay by historian David Hardiman, 'Abkari (tax) came a close second to land revenue in filling colonial coffers and between 1930–31, it yielded 31% (as against land revenue's 41%) of the Madras Presidency's revenues.'[18]

Notwithstanding what it did to the locals, the real object was the revenue – the £5 million raised from the sale of drink, a revenue effortlessly raised and much needed.

While a culture of prodigious drinking had been established in India long before British presence, beginning with the trade with Greece and Rome, the advent of Europeans raised the bar of drinking to another level, bringing into local society the acceptability of social drinking among men and women, rampant bawdiness and drunken behaviour among the foreigners, which found acceptance, as well as the institutionalization of alcohol production and distribution.

Although, as in Britain, the issue of drinking was the subject of various measures related to curbing public disorder and the need for an active Anglo-Indian

Temperance Association, the tax revenues from alcohol supply and sale remained so lucrative that no one paid it particular heed.

Rather, Harry Hobbs, a British army officer who settled in Calcutta to become a very well-known hotelier and memoirist, and others like him continued to see drinking as absolutely essential to living in India, both socially and on account of the hardships that life in the country posed. In a self-published history of Anglo-Indian social life entitled, he wrote: 'How many difficulties have been smoothed over a friendly drink will never be known, nor can it be estimated how much comfort it has given to those depressed by loneliness and over-work in a bad climate.'[19]

Harry Hobbs summarizes it best as he takes stock of his life on the subcontinent: 'Looking back, it hasn't been so bad. I have enjoyed more responsibility than I might ever have hoped for at home; better food and whisky than is generally obtainable in my native land as well as cheap tobacco and servants.'[20]

The general view both in Britain and among the locals in India was that Anglo-Indian society was inherently hedonistic and given to cheerful excesses. In the gymkhana clubs, mess halls, planter bungalows and billiard rooms alcohol flowed freely: gin and punch, brandy and beer and local arrack. No history of the colonies in India is possible without the recognition of the prodigious amount of drinking that took place, where hedonism was not a lapse but a habit.

# 6

# Interdiction and Indulgence: Independence and Beyond

Then, not unexpectedly, at midnight, India gained Independence – free from the shackles of centuries of dominance by the British, Mughals and everyone else who had come to plunder it. Free to explore and find an idiom and identity that was uniquely Indian. Unprepared and inexperienced, weighed down by the expectations and aspirations of millions, India took its first tentative steps towards determining Indianness. Not an easy task in the face of illiteracy, unemployment, inequality and lack of infrastructure. Despite abject poverty and food shortages, India's dependency on alcohol did not decline; rather, it persisted and even worsened in some areas. Drinking became a way to negotiate hardship rather than a vice to be abandoned.

There was certainly no independence from liquor.

Changing social norms, a rising middle class and liberalization had Indian manufacturers setting up modern distilleries, experimenting with ageing processes, blending and using local ingredients. From colonial dependency to postcolonial interdiction and ambivalence, India has risen to become not just the world's largest consumer of spirits but a world-class producer of some of the most globally celebrated spirits.

There is a sea of red lights as cars carrying weary office goers slowly inch their way home back towards Gurugram. Once you cross the bottleneck at the toll gates, you are immediately dazzled by the hallmark high-rise buildings, neon signs of multinational companies, glass-fronted facades and brightly lit offices that make up Gurugram. In the midst of this concrete jungle are pockets of even brighter shops that probably attract more people than the offices. Swanky and well-designed, with dazzling lights and shiny glass shelves stocked with sparkling bottles, these are the famed and ubiquitous booze shops of Gurugram stocked with the best-priced liquor in all of India.

This a symbol of the new India: youthful, unapologetic and triumphant, proud of all that it has been able to achieve. It is a celebration – of hard work and a good life well earned. Restaurants and bars abound in a town filled with numerous global companies that employ a young work force, gathering to have a much-deserved beer at the end of the day; groups of young girls sit around largely unharassed having their vodkas and grab a bite before going back to their shared apartments. Neeraj Sachdeva, the US-educated owner of numerous Lakeview liquor stores that dot Haryana says, 'There is a lot of ease about buying booze these days … nothing surreptitious about it – even women come now into our shops without hesitation to buy liquor, something that was unheard of. The shops are like huge departmental stores and we employ a number of floor shop girls so that they feel very comfortable.'[1]

It's not just the locals who come a-visiting. Sachdeva says that they now have something called alcohol tourism, with, on an average, at least 30 people coming every day from far-flung cities like Hyderabad, Bengaluru and Chennai to buy their tipple.

The enthusiasm is catching. The drinking culture that thrives around the world has come to India too – the statistics are astounding. The BBC claims India to be the largest consumer of whisky worldwide with an annual consumption of 663 million litres.[2] So it's not just glitzy Gurugram – there is Bengaluru, home to United Breweries that set up pubs in the early 80s; there are micro-breweries in Chennai, restaurants in Mumbai, clubs in Kolkata and bars in Goa and numerous smaller towns. India is drinking all over again.

But with a difference.

To begin with, the average age of people buying alcohol and frequenting these places has dropped considerably. While the legal age for sale and consumption of alcohol varies from state to state, ranging anywhere between 18 and 25, no one is really checking. With only four states, Bihar, Gujarat, Nagaland and Mizoram, imposing prohibition and declaring themselves to be 'dry', the rest go from liberal to conservate depending on their vote banks and fiscal needs.

It wasn't always so. The role of Mahatma Gandhi in bringing about Independence is well documented; less well known is his commitment to bringing temperance to Independent India. A lifelong teetotaller, Gandhi, especially seeing the staggering quantities of liquor consumed in British India, was determined to make prohibition a priority of the government, a goal that resulted in the inclusion of prohibition into India's first

Constitution in 1949. Having experienced first-hand the effects of alcohol on people across the country, especially the poor and dispossessed, he argued that 'the one thing most deplorable next to untouchability is the drink curse'.[3]

An aversion to alcohol was a key Gandhian tenet, so much so that it was included in the Directive Principles of State Policy. However, banning alcohol was not a prerogative of the central government; each state had its own power to decide its liquor policies. The depleted state of the exchequer post-Independence was a key reason not to impose prohibition, as the excise duties imposed on liquor did not just provide significant revenues but, in many cases, were the highest revenue earner in a state. Ironically, prohibition provided a large vote bank as the poorer section of women wanted temperance imposed because their men squandered away household money on liquor, resulting in abuse, rape and crime. Caught in the middle, state governments to date vacillate depending on political expediency.

A case in point is glittering Gurugram. In 1996, the Haryana Vikas Party, led by freedom fighter Bansi Lal, led a campaign with a promise to ban alcohol if elected. Lal won the chief minister's seat and delivered on his promise, only to find to his great chagrin that there was a thriving cross-border mafia that smuggled in liquor in humungous quantities – women pretending to be pregnant, children carrying illicit bottles in their schoolbags, milkmen spiking their milk with liquor – resulting in a loss of over ₹1,200 crore in revenue, which had to be covered by raising taxes on essential goods. This in turn resulted in him losing the national elections in 1998. Things got so bad that the high court instituted a commission to investigate the aftermath of the prohibition rules. It indicted Bansi Lal and his son for 'creating a situation for smuggling of liquor', with Lal himself admitting that there was a large liquor mafia at work.[4]

Probably the most confused state that is constantly getting on and off the liquor wagon is Tamil Nadu. It consumes liquor in such copious quantities that successive governments have been loath to take a permanent stand on the liquor policy. Prohibition has a long and tumultuous history in Tamil Nadu, with alcohol first being banned in 1937, after the Congress won the election for the first legislative assembly in the British-ruled Madras Presidency. C. Rajagopalachari, its first chief minister, banned liquor throughout the state. The period of prohibition under Rajagopalachari turned out to be the longest one in the state, lasting until 1971 when the new Dravida Munnetra Kazhagam (DMK) government decided to lift prohibition.

Appalled, Rajagopalachari, whose life mission had been to ensure temperance among Tamils, hurried to meet Chief Minister M. Karunanidhi to dissuade him. 'An aging Rajaji, with all the melodrama of a Tamil film, drove to Karunanidhi's home in pouring rain to dissuade him but was met with a metaphorical reply: Tamil Nadu was "a lump of camphor amidst a ring of fire" said the erudite film script writer turned chief minister Karunanidhi.'[5] In other words, when liquor flowed freely in the neighbouring states, how could Tamil Nadu stay dry? Karunanidhi released Tamils from a quarter of a century of prohibition.

It was short-lived though. Two years later, the government banned toddy shops once again and soon imposed total prohibition, first of arrack and then of Indian-made foreign liquor (IMFL). Only permit-holders who had medical certificates proving that they could not do without alcohol were permitted to purchase IMFL. There are numerous humorous stories about the long queues outside doctors' clinics as people lined up for their permits that declared them to be alcoholics.

As liquor consumption went underground, bootlegging spiked, leading to massive deaths due to spurious liquor consumption.

Liquor policies changed with every new government. When M.G. Ramachandran came to power, he lifted the prohibition, only to have his successor Jayalalithaa promise to reintroduce prohibition if re-elected. Finally, in 2003, the AIADMK decided to bring IMFL retail back, but under the control of the state. The Tamil Nadu State Marketing Corporation (TASMAC), which had until then been working as a wholesale trader, now staged a coup of sorts and took over more than 7,000 liquor shops across the state. It is now the only retailer of IMFL, which has enabled it to provide a fifth of the state's revenue. This policy, as the Tamil Nadu Commissionerate of Prohibition and Excise notes in its history of the flip-flops, 'continues till date'.

Imposing sweeping prohibition policies has proved difficult in the long run, as many states have found out. Kerala, a state that draws much of its revenue from tourism, for instance, thought it would bridge the gap between total prohibition and an open policy by imposing a partial ban on the sale of alcohol, but it led to further confusion: Only wine and beer bars could operate while all hard liquor was banned, a move that again resulted in losing an election.

So, the saga continues as states caught between revenue and remorse continue to vacillate, indicative of the absence of core beliefs. Out of all the states, Arunachal Pradesh has the highest proportion of both men (53 per cent) and women (24 per cent) who drink alcohol, followed by Telangana (43 per cent men), Sikkim (16 per cent women), Assam, districts in Jharkhand and Chhattisgarh, Odisha, Haryana, Tamil Nadu – in short, everyone.[6]

Banning alcohol in India is economically devastating to the states as well as the pockets of politicians – liquor scams abound; almost every state has had one. Prohibition is packaged in the garb of saving people's lives, but politicians have one eye on the vote bank and the other on the exchequer, with concerns about people's health and alcohol-induced road accidents, violence and rape being easily relegated to the bin. It is hypocrisy at its worst, but it is not just politics – alcohol and duplicity have gone hand in hand in India since the very beginning.

Drinking from the earliest times was segregated by caste and class – who could drink, how much and where, with the penalties for drinking also varying from class to class. Up until a few decades ago (and in many communities even today) marriage proposals were usually accompanied with a list of questions: apart from caste and money considerations, the questionnaire usually centred around whether the groom-to-be had any 'bad habits' – did he smoke, did he drink, did he gamble? (Sex didn't matter.) Tick any of these boxes and the proposal was binned.

Drinking at home is taboo even today for the average Indian, seen as a violation of honour and respect. Young men are expected to never drink in front of their fathers and elders, as it is viewed as a sign of disrespect. Naveen Kumar, 36, a father of two and a physiotherapist from Haryana, says he has never had a drink with his father, an army officer who has a drink every day: 'It would be seen as extreme disrespect if I had a drink with my father or other older men of the family. He even refused to hand over a bottle of rum to me saying that he'd never give a bottle of alcohol to his son with his own hands.'[7] This attitude notwithstanding, in the Haryana village that Naveen comes from most men drink – some excessively, others moderately, but drinking is de rigueur.

Come 6.00 p.m. and the government-controlled metal-cage-like shuttered liquor shops have long queues of people jostling to buy booze; they then retire to the nearest park and gulp down a few pegs quickly before wending their way home. Before the recent boom of bars and restaurants, drinking in India, like smoking and sex, was furtive, something to be done surreptitiously in dark corners. Parking lots and park benches were the preferred places for a rendezvous, to drink and hold hands until the beat cops arrived to chase you away. Even early bars and pubs, far from being social places where people could relax, meet friends and colleagues, were no better than dingy dhabas where the lighting was deliberately kept dim to ensure people wouldn't recognize each other. Women, even those accompanied by men, were frowned upon. The only time when drinking was openly encouraged by families was during the wedding season, especially among the Punjabis, for whom it was tradition to goad the groom and his friends to continue drinking and dancing until the groom was inebriated enough to get married. Largely thanks to Karan Johar's films, the more sedate South Indians too have started having mehendi and sangeet ceremonies where drinking, until now completely taboo, is slowly gathering acceptance.

Indian cinema has always been a good index and chronicler of social norms, and the way in which it has portrayed alcohol over the years is a good indicator of changing times. In Indian cinema, alcohol has always had a moral subtext, with drinking seldom being a social activity or an act of fun; drinking is loaded with symbolism, conveying depravity, depression, angst or a life gone astray, especially when it comes to women. While the gap between women and men is narrowing, the percentage of women who drink is still very small, but the reaction evoked by it is intense. There is something about women drinking that continues to rile men, the question of morality immediately raising its head especially with regards to sex. The idea that drinking leads to the loosening of inhibitions, followed by sex, is very deeply embedded in the psyche of men and is a part of our popular culture.

Cinema audiences have for decades watched women being divided into two categories, saintly virginal heroines in white sarees and long-sleeved blouses pitted against sexily clad bad girls who smoked, drank and danced in discos. One of the first movies to depict depression and alcoholism was the classic film *Sahib Bibi aur Ghulam* from 1963, in which Chhoti Bahu takes to drink to entice her wayward husband, gradually sliding into an alcoholic stupor, only to be further rejected by her husband who finds her drinking unworthy of a woman of her class. The character was played by Meena Kumari, who had problems with alcohol herself. Then of course there was Parveen Babi's character in *Deewaar* (1975), in which she plays a prostitute who gets pregnant. Babi is murdered in the film, meeting that brutal fate always meted out to 'loose' women. In *Arth* (1982), Smita Patil plays Kavita, an actor who likes a drink, breaks up a marriage and finally crumbles in distress. But the queen of bad women in Hindi cinema is of course Helen Richardson Khan, simply known as 'Helen', whose signature moves are a hallmark of the sexiest Bollywood songs of the 1960s and 1970s. Aside from dancing with wild abandon, Helen poured men drinks, often blew cigarette smoke into their faces and seduced them. But cinema too has changed – in the past decade, it seems to have decided that women who enjoy a drink are actually cool. Now, according to film wisdom, alcohol and cigarettes have become code for independence, sassiness or liberated women.

It was no different for the men, who were separated into either heroes or Vat 69-drinking villains. The brand was synonymous with Bollywood baddies. Amitabh Bachchan's character in *Don* (1978), an underworld boss, finds comfort in the amber liquid. Other older villains played by Pran, Prem Chopra or Ajit chugged whole bottles of it while sprouting ridiculous dialogues and then rushing to rape the heroine. And then there are movies like *Devdas* (1955), based on the 1917 novel by Sarat Chandra Chattopadhyay, centred on unrequited love, a theme that found much favour among film producers, giving rise to many a drunken scene. Who can forget Dharmendra's drunken scene in *Sholay* (1975) where he threatens to commit suicide? Less stigmatized than women drinking, men drinking is often depicted as a coping mechanism to deal with grief and loss.

If cinema has changed dramatically, becoming less moralistic and moving away from traditional melodrama and rigid moral strictures to exploring contemporary social realities, so has life. Along with other things, drinking has come to be seen as conducive to social interaction, not necessarily leading to moral depravity and addiction. More and more it is becoming an accepted form of social behaviour, of communication, if you will – an easy way to relax, share an evening and communicate without awkwardness. This social acceptance of drinking has led to alcohol making its appearance at all celebrations: weddings, parties, brunches, lunches and, as is common in many countries, for an after-work downtime drink. Even the taboo of women drinking in public is fast disappearing with women now forming a significant part of the alcohol consumer base.

As with much else in India, it has to do with the population, or rather the excess of it. India has approximately 10–12 million people reaching the legal drinking age annually, and with a median age of 29, it is one of the youngest populations globally, making it a fabulous market for alcohol manufacturers. A large part of these huge numbers has come from people who previously eschewed alcohol and have been impacted by dramatic social changes in attitude and behaviour. Much has changed, from the kind of people who drink to what, where and how they are drinking, as well as socio-economic changes brought about by social media, education, urbanization and a rising middle class. These have changed the social fabric of society, reversing centuries of superstition, class segregation, religious traditions, hypocrisy and moral rectitude. Social drinking has become a normal and acceptable behaviour in popular culture.

In keeping with its new confident image, India is ready and excited to experiment, driven by a growing young and adventurous consumer base. These young drinkers have gone from being surreptitious drinkers to tastemakers, setting new trends in what is being drunk, where and why. Gone are the days of Vat 69, Johnnie Walker Red Label and Old Monk; in their place has arrived a whole array of whisky, gin, vodka and other drinks that local alcohol manufacturers have woken up to. With people demanding variety, willing to experiment with diverse flavours and new exotic drinks, the market is soaring.

India is soon to take over as one of the world's largest at-home consumer markets, a unique driver for consumers to pay attention to their home bars and hosting experiences in individualistic spaces. Even as restaurants, lounge bars and taverns are springing up at alarming speed, homes are now being designed with bars and wine cellars in mind. Gone are the days when *paua* bottles were hidden under the kitchen sink; men are enthusiastically collecting and displaying their bottles, from vintage wine to expensive malt whisky and trending tequila. Dinner parties where wine is paired with food are no longer just restricted to Michelin-starred restaurants, they are happening at homes, with talented mixologists and culinary pros experimenting with exclusive degustation menus, giving rise to new vocabulary, alternative careers and even alcohol influencers.

These contemporary consumers will soon become the biggest buyers of luxury brands by far, representing 80 per cent of global purchases, an astonishing figure. According to Euromonitor International, India's luxury market is expected to be one of the fastest growing in the world, with fine spirits contributing to a large segment of luxury consumption. India is now one of the largest importers of premium liquor, particularly Scotch and fine wines, with imports valued at over US $1 billion annually, reflecting a growing appetite for quality beverages. According to Future Market Insights, India's alcohol market is projected to be valued at $200 billion by 2025 and forecasted to grow to an estimated value of $300 billion between 2025 and 2035.[8] Supported by a rising middle class and increased consumer spending on premium, experiential activities.

The alcohol economy in India is robust and is catching the attention of the world market. A recent report by International Wine and Spirits Record (IWSR), a leading global authority on international alcohol industry data, estimates that the Indian alcohol market has emerged as the fastest growing alcohol market in the world topping the list of 20 major economies for three consecutive years.[9] This will add an incremental value of approximately US $7.6 billion over the next four years until 2028, which is as much as what the US market will add over the same period. Putting it simply, in 2022 India bought 219 million bottles of Scotch whisky – and yes, Johnnie Walker continues its domination of the Indian whisky palate.

But local manufacturers have not been sitting on their haunches either. The last decade has seen an upsurge in the number of Indian brands entering top 10 lists in categories that were otherwise dominated by international brands. Amrut and Paul John were the first Indian single-malt brands, and in the past few years, there has been a flurry of new single-malt distillers, including Piccadily Agro, which launched Indri and Kamet, and Radico Khaitan with its Rampur – brands that have found a place even in international markets. Rampur Asava was recognized as the Best World Whisky in 2023. According to the IWSR, an alcohol market researcher, Indian single malts outsold their Scotch counterparts in 2024.[10]

It is not just the Scotch market that is growing. Fuelled by a growing number of women drinking, a vibrant restaurant, bar and cocktail scene too is growing, contributing to the popularity of gin, vodka and tequila being projected to reach sales of US $1.8 billion in the coming years. The botanical complexity of gin and innovative mixologists who blend in local tastes have led to a surging market. Curiosity is the big driver of India's consumption: The import of wine and sake is also increasing astronomically this year, alongside the rise in craft beer sales.

But it is not just about premium brands and malt whiskies; nationalism is also showing up in alcohol manufacturing. There is a growing appreciation for craft beverages, and the stigma that 'desi' equals '*adda* and low-quality' is fading. Another emerging trend is that of country liquor, such as *tongba* (Sikkim, Darjeeling), *judima* (Assam) and *sekmai yu* (Manipur) among others, finding spots on local bar menus. Feni, a country liquor native to Goa, made from fermented cashew, often dismissed as smelly and relegated to local bars, is now found in almost every bar across the state. The reason is a rise in demand, so much so that there is an annual feni festival organized every year by the Goa Department of Tourism, which boasts a feni experience centre along with mixology classes.

The other fascinating story is of mahua, a heritage spirit that was unfairly sidelined during the colonial era to make way for imported spirits. Made of bright red flowers that were gathered and distilled by tribal women to supplement their household incomes, the rather raw distil is a spirit deeply rooted in India's history. Central to festivals, marriages and community gatherings, mahua was considered to be sacred and have medicinal properties. This spirit is finally finding its place in the sun largely due to the efforts of people like Desmond Nazareth, managing director of Agave India, whose mission is to transform mahua into a heritage luxury craft spirit. And it's working – strong branding and compelling narratives are helping Indian spirits gain prominence and reach a broader audience beyond niche circles.

The past few decades have seen unprecedented changes in how India lives and perceives itself. Driven by technology, social media, economic growth and education, the cultural and social transformations have been dramatic, largely propelled by a young population. This cultural shift has opened doors for brands to engage with a broader demographic, catering to a more inclusive audience. These young consumers drive demand for more sophisticated drinking experiences, favouring craft cocktails, upscale venues, and premium products.

There is an increasing number of women participating in social drinking, spurring the demand for varied product offerings. United Breweries Group, a subsidiary of The Heineken Company, unveiled a limited-edition beer called Queenfisher: The Queen of Good Times, envisioned as an all-women initiative – celebrating women and sisterhood, championing inclusivity, while challenging the accepted norm that enjoying beer was the prerogative of only one gender. A decade ago, women drank fruit-flavoured drinks like Breezer, laden with sugar and synthetic flavours and coloured with artificial ingredients. Today, around 40 per cent of the beer consumed in metros and close to 60 per cent of the cocktails ordered in bars are bought by women.[11]

Younger generations, led by millennials and the Gen Z, are a revolving door of new-age consumption trends, as they learn new buying behaviour every month. New brands showcase the new confident India that is proud of creating its own palate. A newcomer to the alcohol business, Uppal Breweries & Distillers has launched a 100-crore ambitious plan to launch a premium product every six months. It has done so by introducing Madhvan, a well-priced whisky in an Indian avatar. The company found a cultural niche, as the name 'Madhvan' implies a blend of *madhu* (honey) and *van* (forest). The whisky also carries other Indian symbols, like the logo of a leaping tiger and a very filmy tag line (*dahaad iraado ki* [the roar of the unshakeable will]). This is a totally homegrown, made in India product.

The most obvious outcome of all this is that after almost 2,000 years of drinking, whether ceremonially, as medicine or just out of abject penury, Indians have finally begun to understand the need to drink responsibly. The days of *daaru pee kar nautanki karna* or 'creating a ruckus under the influence of alcohol' are fading away. Even among the young, the era of grabbing the cheapest and quickest way to get high and behaving erratically, often leading to violent brawls, embarrassing moments or unwanted pregnancies, is now a thing of the past. Blending in gender stereotypes, the juvenile competition of 'how many drinks can one hold' is increasingly frowned upon.

Generalizations are odious and difficult, especially in a country like India, but there appears to be a shift in drinking patterns even among the young. The emphasis on fitness, body image and wellness has seen people moving away from heavy drinking in favour of more mindful consumption, with importance being given to experiences, well-being and fun social engagement. Today's youth are more likely to drink in moderation, showcasing a desire for sophistication rather than excess.

This generational change is further reflected in the rising popularity of alcohol-free alternatives like kombucha and mocktails. The youth aspire to remain sober and in control during social gatherings, fostering connections that are deeper and more meaningful. Oversimplifications are generally misleading; nonetheless, young people today surprisingly appear as more responsible drinkers than their parents and grandparents. They pace their drinks better, exercise moderation and prioritize experiences over excess.

From toddy to tequila, the landscape of drinking in India has seen a seismic shift in tradition and culture, from the quality of what the people drink to where and how they consume liquor. Today, India's indigenous liquor sector stands proudly at the crossroads of tradition and modernity, making some of the world's best liquor while both reflecting pride in India's diverse heritage and upholding world-class quality.

# Acknowledgements

This book was written to sneak in a bit of history in a format that was more palatable … so alcohol it was. The amount of research, documents, papers and books that are available on the subject speaks of the interest that alcohol has evoked through millennia. My gratitude goes to the many, many scholars, translators, researchers and storytellers whose insights have made this book possible.

Also, my heartfelt thanks to my family and friends who opened up their bars to ease the writing, my editors at Juggernaut, and a special thanks to Anuj Bahri.

# Notes

## 1. Euphoric Beginnings: Soma and Sura

1. J.L. Shastri and G.V. Tagare (eds), *The Narada-Purana Part 3*, Ancient Indian Tradition and Mythology Vol. 17, Motilal Banarsidass, 1952.
2. H.H. Wilson (trans.), *Rgveda Samhita Vol. 3*, Motilal Banarsidass, [1866].
3. Arthur Berriedale Keith (trans.), *Rigveda Brahmanas: The Aitareya and Kausitaki Brahmanas of the Rigveda*, Motilal Baransidass, 1988, p. 128.
4. Ralph T.H. Griffith (trans.), *The Hymns of the Rig Veda*, Vol. 1, 2nd Edition, E.J. Lazarus and Co., Benares, 1896.
5. Swami Vijnanananda (trans.), *Devi Bhagavata Purana*, Vol. 2, Allahabad, Motilal Benarsidass, 1922.
6. Ralph T.H. Griffith (trans.), *The Rig Veda,* 1896, https://tinyurl.com/yj3tzp67, accessed 20 November 2025.
7. Ibid.
8. A.L. Basham, *The Wonder That Was India: A Survey of the Culture of the Indian Sub-Continent Before the Coming*

*of the Muslims*, Sidgwick & Jackson, 1954.
9. Ralph T.H. Griffith (trans.), *The Rig Veda*, 1896, https://tinyurl.com/yj3tzp67, accessed 20 November 2025.
10. Frederick Eden Pargiter (trans.), *Markandeya Purana*, Motilal Banarsidass, 1904.
11. G.V. Tagare (trans.), *The Brahmanda Purana Part 5: Lalita-Mahatamya*, Ancient Indian Traditions and Mythology, Vol. 22, J.L. Shastri, G.P. Bhatt and G.V. Tagare (eds), Motilal Banarsidass, [1958].
12. Rekha Rao, 'Vajapeya Yagna', *Academia.edu*, https://tinyurl.com/287dh4kk, accessed 21 November 2022.
13. Ralph T.H. Griffith (trans.), *The Rig Veda*, 1896, https://tinyurl.com/yj3tzp67, accessed 20 November 2025.
14. G.V. Tagare (trans.), *The Brahmanda Purana Part 5: Lalita-Mahatamya*, Ancient Indian Traditions and Mythology, Vol. 22, J.L. Shastri, G.P. Bhatt and G.V. Tagare (eds), Motilal Banarsidass, [1958].
15. Desiraju Hanumanta Rao (trans.), *Valmiki Ramayana*, https://tinyurl.com/mr3kmrhv, accessed 21 November 2025.
16. J.L. Shastri and G.V. Tagare (eds), *The Narada-Purana Part 3*, Ancient Indian Tradition and Mythology Vol. 17, Motilal Banarsidass, 1952.
17. G.V. Tagare (ed.), *The Vayu Purana Part 1*, Ancient Indian Tradition and Mythology Vol. 37, J.L. Shastri, G.P. Bhatt and G.V. Tagare (eds), Motilal Banarsidass, Delhi, 1960.
18. *Free Press Journal*, 14 October 2021.

19. 'The Divine Drunkard 1', *Haasyarasa*, 26 June 2017, https://tinyurl.com/4wxu7da7, accessed 25 November 2025.
20. Manmatha Nath Dutt (trans.), *Harivamsha Purana*, Motilal Banarsidass, [1897].
21. G.V. Tagare (trans.), *The Skanda Purana Part 1*, Ancient Indian Tradition and Mythology, Vol. 49, J.L. Shastri, G.P. Bhatt, N.A. Deshpande (eds), Motilal Banarsidass, 1950.
22. Swami Vijnanananda (trans.), *Devi Bhagavata Purana*, Vol. 1, Allahabad, Motilal Benarsidass, 1922.
23. J.L. Shastri (ed.), *The Siva Purana Part 1*, Ancient Indian Tradition and Mythology, Vol. 1, J.L. Shastri (ed.), Motilal Banarsidass, 1950.
24. Harinder Singh Khaira, 'Devotees Offer 25,000 Bottles of Liquor at Kali Temple in Patiala', *Hindustan Times*, 17 April 2016, https://tinyurl.com/4uwcy9xu, accessed 21 November 2025.
25. K.S. Bhagwan, *Rama Mandiru Yeke Beda*, Ladai Prakashana, 2018.
26. Desiraju Hanumanta Rao (trans.), *Valmiki Ramayana*, https://tinyurl.com/mr3kmrhv, accessed 21 November 2025.
27. Ibid.
28. N.A. Deshpande (trans.), *The Padma Purana Part 6,* Ancient Indian Tradition and Mythology, Vol. 39, J.L. Shastri, G.P. Bhatt, N.A. Deshpande (eds), Motilal Banarsidass, 1951.

29. Kisari Mohan Ganguli (trans.), *The Mahabharata of Krishna-Dwaipanya Vyasa*, Motilal Banarsidass, 2013.
30. G.V. Tagare (trans.), 'Book 7, Section 1, Chapter 101', *Skanda Purana,* Vol. 67, Ancient Indian Tradition and Mythology, J.L. Shastri, G.P. Bhatt and N.A. Deshpande (eds), Motilal Banarsidass, 1950.
31. Sudhakar Malaviya (trans.), *Gobhila ka Gryhya Sutra*, Chaukhamba Publishers, 2019.
32. Ralph T.H. Griffins (trans.), *The Hymns of the Atharvaveda*, E.J. Lazarus and Co., 1917.
33. Moti Chandra, *Kashi ka Itihaas*, University Publications and Aastha Prakashan Mandir, 1962.
34. Sri Rama Ramanuja Acari (ed.), *Apastamba Dharma & Grihya Sutras*, https://tinyurl.com/bdh47b44, accessed 11 December 2025.
35. Ganganath Jha (ed.), *Manusmriti with the Commentary of Medhatithi*, Motilal Banarsidass, 1920.
36. Ibid.
37. Nathan, 'Intoxicant Consumption in Hinduism Series | Part 5: Hindu Scriptures on Liquor Drinking', *Answering Hinduism*, 30 September 2020, https://tinyurl.com/2n32n3xb, accessed 24 November 2025.
38. H.H. Wilson (trans). *Rig-Veda Sanhita: A Collection of Ancient Hindu Hymns*, The Bengaluru Printing & Publishing Co. Ltd, 1926, p. 239.
39. Ganganath Jha (ed.), *Manusmriti with the Commentary of Medhatithi*, Motilal Banarsidass, 1920.
40. Ibid.

41. Ottilingam Somasundaram, D. Vijaya Raghavan and A.G. Tejus Murthy, 'Drinking Habits in Ancient India', *Indian Journal of Psychiatry*, vol. 58, no. 1, 2016, pp. 93–6, https://doi.org/ 10.4103/0019-5545.174396.

## 2. Nirvana and Wellness: The Middle Path

1. Bhikkhu Bodhi, 'A Discipline of Sobriety', *Access to Insight: Readings in Theravada Buddhism*, 1998, https://tinyurl.com/5n8y7tp6, accessed 4 December 2025.
2. E.B. Cowell (ed.), 'No. 512', *The Jataka or Stories of The Buddha's Former Births*, Volume 5, Cambridge University Press, 1905.
3. Ibid.
4. E.B. Cowell (ed.), *The Jataka or Stories of The Buddha's Former Births*, Volume 1, Cambridge University Press, 1905.
5. Chenco Dorji, 'The Myth behind Alcohol Happiness', *Proceedings of the Second International Conference on Gross National Happiness*, 2005, https://tinyurl.com/yuf6y4yn, accessed 25 November 2025.
6. Gyurme Dorje, 'Introduction', *Guhyagarbha Tantra*, 1987, https://tinyurl.com/kpvffjxj, accessed 4 December 2025.
7 Rohini Swamy, 'It's Alcohol and It's Ayurvedic — How Kerala Drinkers Are Beating Booze Lockdown', *ThePrint*, 1 May 2020, https://tinyurl.com/3z88xc6t, accessed 25 November 2025.

8. Kaviraj Kunja Lal Bhishagratna (ed.), 'Chapter XLVII – Symptoms and Treatment of Alcoholism (Panatyaya)', *Sushruta Samhita, Volume 6: Uttara-Tantra*, Motilal Banarsidass, 1916.
9. Ibid.
10. Ibid.
11. Ibid.
12. P.V. Sharma (trans.), 'Chapter 24', *Charak Samhita (Text with English Translation)*, Chaukhamba Oreintalia, 2005, pp. 62–9.

## 3. Spirited South: Southern Libertines

1. Zac O'Yeah, 'The Unlikely Treasures of Arikamedu', *Mint*, 13 May 2018, https://tinyurl.com/pb4jt4xz, accessed 21 November 2025.
2. 'Finding an Amphora in Arikamedu', *The Hindu*, 3 February 2019, https://tinyurl.com/msbbzj2d, accessed 21 November 2025.
3. Srinivas Reddy, 'Vijayanagara Was More Magnificent than Rome, and Krishnadevaraya India's First Global Leader', *ThePrint*, 20 May 2020, https://tinyurl.com/4y4zrdfs, accessed 3 December 2025.
4. A.K. Ramanujan, *Poems of Love and War*, Columbia University Press, 1985.
5. George L. Hart and Hank Heifetz (trans, eds), *The Four Hundred Songs of War and Wisdom: An Anthology of Poems from Classical Tamil, the Purananuru: Translations*

*from the Asian Classics*, Columbia University Press, 2002.

6. Ibid.
7. V.R. Devika, 'What Avvai Meant to Women', *The Hindu*, 28 June 2018, https://tinyurl.com/ys7ev9yz,, accessed 21 November 2025.
8. Ibid.
9. Ibid.
10. J.V. Chelliah (trans.), *Pattupattu: Ten Tamil Idylls*, General Publishers, 1975.
11. Ibid.
12. A.R. Venkatachalapathy, 'Camphor in a Ring of Fire', *The Hindu*, 16 November 2021, https://tinyurl.com/yyt8e229, accessed 25 November 2025.
13. Jyotsana Kamat, 'Drinking in Ancient Karnataka', *Kamat's Potpourri*, 2025, https://tinyurl.com/ymt37kta, accessed on 21 November 2025.
14. Ibid.
15. Ibid.
16. Chaitanya Chinta, 'Witness to Glory: Domingo Paes and the Vijayanagara Empire', *Medium*, 4 August 2023, https://tinyurl.com/3h6xyezk, accessed on 3 December 2025.
17. Raoul McLaughlin, *Rome and the Distant East: Trade Routes to the Ancient Lands of Arabia, India and China*, Hambledon Continuum, 2010, pp. 48–50.
18. Marco Polo, *The Travels of Marco Polo, the Venetian: The Translation of Marsden*, G. Bell and Sons, 1892, pp. 370–1.

19. 'Chapter 93: Avoiding Alcohol', Thirukkural in English: A Modern Rendition of the Tamil Classic, 2016, https://tinyurl.com/w4383p6v, accessed 4 December 2025.
20. Sunitha Natti, 'Which Indian States Spend the Most on Liquor? A New Study Attempts to Give the Answer', *The New Indian Express*, 24 August 2024, https://tinyurl.com/bdcnhwet, accessed 4 December 2025.

## 4. Mughal Majesty: Hedonism and Piety

1. Mark Cartwright, 'Food & Drink in the Mongol Empire', *World History Encyclopedia*, 26 September 2019, https://tinyurl.com/2462z4a9, accessed 20 November 2025.
2. Mohammed Maraqten, 'Wine Drinking and Wine Prohibition in Arabia before Islam', *Proceedings of the Seminar for Arabic Studies*, vol. 23, 1993, pp. 95–115, https://tinyurl.com/kpzba7mw, accessed 25 November 2025.
3. Ibid.
4. Stephanie Honchell, 'Pursuing Pleasure, Attaining Oblivion: The Roles and Uses of Intoxicants at the Mughal Court', Paper 628, *Electronic Theses and Dissertations*, 2010, https://doi.org/10.18297/etd/628.
5. Haroon Asghar, 'Islam and Psychedelics: An Essay on the Issues of Permissibility and Medical Utility',

*Theology and Science*, vol. 23, no. 2, 2025, pp. 344–78, https://doi.org/10.1080/14746700.2025.2472125.

6. Imran Ahsan Khan Nyazee, *Islamic Jurisprudence: Usul al-Fiqh*, CreateSpace Independent Publishing Platform, 2016.
7. John Andrew Morrow, *Islamic Images and Ideas: Essays on Sacred Symbolism,* McFarland, 2013, pp. 83.
8. Ibid.
9. Najam Haider, 'Contesting Intoxication: Early Juristic Debates over the Lawfulness of Alcoholic Beverages', *Islamic Law and Society*, Brill, 2013, pp. 48–89, https://tinyurl.com/5fr2xp5s, accessed on 20 November 2025.
10. Stephanie Honchell, 'Pursuing Pleasure, Attaining Oblivion: The Roles and Uses of Intoxicants at the Mughal Court', Paper 628, *Electronic Theses and Dissertations*, 2010, https://doi.org/10.18297/etd/628.
11. Stephanie Honchell, 'The Story of a Drunken Mughal: Islam, Alcohol, and Imperial Ambition', *Social History of Alcohol and Drugs*, vol. 29, 2015, pp. 4–28, https://tinyurl.com/4dsn9s6z, accessed 4 December 2025; Rizwan Ahmad and Rekha Pande, 'Role of Wine in Mughal Socio-Political Sphere: A Historical Analysis', *Retrospect: Peer-Reviewed Academic Journal of Archaeology, Anthropology, History and Heritage Tourism*, 2023, https://tinyurl.com/25m8nbmn, accessed 11 December 2025.
12. Wheeler M. Thackston (ed.), *The Baburnama: Memoirs of Babur, Prince and Emperor,* Oxford University Press, 1996.

13. Stephen F. Dale, *The Garden of Eight Paradises*, Brill's Inner Asian Library, 2004. p. 312.
14. Stephanie Honchell, 'The Story of a Drunken Mughal: Islam, Alcohol, and Imperial Ambition', *Social History of Alcohol and Drugs*, vol. 29, 2015, pp. 4–28, https://tinyurl.com/4dsn9s6z, accessed 4 December 2025.
15. Wheeler M. Thackston (ed.), *The Baburnama: Memoirs of Babur, Prince and Emperor*, Oxford University Press, 1996.
16. Stephanie Honchell, 'The Story of a Drunken Mughal: Islam, Alcohol, and Imperial Ambition', *Social History of Alcohol and Drugs*, vol. 29, 2015, pp. 4–28, https://tinyurl.com/4dsn9s6z, accessed 4 December 2025.
17. Stephanie Honchell, 'Pursuing Pleasure, Attaining Oblivion: The Roles and Uses of Intoxicants at the Mughal Court', Paper 628, Electronic Theses and Dissertations, 2010, https://doi.org/10.18297/etd/628.
18. John Leyden and William Erskine (trans), *Memoirs of Zehir-Ed-Din Muhammed Babur*, 2 Vols, Oxford University Press, London, 1921.
19. Promod Sangar, 'Drinking in Medieval India', *The Tribune – Saturday Plus*, 31 October 1998, https://tinyurl.com/yp3np923, accessed 4 December 2025.
20. Goldie Francis, *The First Christian Mission to the Great Mogul, or, The Story of Blessed Rudolf Acquaviva: and of His Four Companions in Martyrdom of the Society of Jesus*, M.H. Gill, Dublin, 1897.
21. Ibid.

22. G. Singh and B. Lal, 'Culture and Alcohol – Cultural Traditions and Alcohol Consumption in India', *Comparative Medicine East and West*, vol. 6, no. 3, 1979, pp. 229–36; Saji Joseph and Hemlata K., 'Alcohol and Alcoholism in India; A Historical Review', *International Journal of Science and Healthcare Research*, vol. 5, no. 4, 2020, pp. 343–54.
23. Ziya us Salam, 'What Baburnama Says', *The Frontline*, 21 November 2019, https://tinyurl.com/mcm5mjh7, accessed on 4 December 2025.
24. Henry Beveridge (ed.), *The Tuzuk-i-Jahangiri; or, Memoirs of Jahangir*, Alexander Rogers (trans.), London Royal Asiatic Society, 1909–14.
25. Parvati Sharma, *Jahangir: An Intimate Portrait of a Great Mughal*, Juggernaut Books, 2018.
26. Ibid.
27. Ibid.
28. Ibid.
29. G. Shreekumar Menon, 'Infatuation, Inebriation and Intoxication of a Mughal King', *Mangalore Today*, 10 January 2019, https://tinyurl.com/yc3uwnk6, accessed 4 December 2025.
30. Parvati Sharma, *Jahangir: An Intimate Portrait of a Great Mughal*, Juggernaut Books, 2018.
31. G. ShreeKumar Menon, 'Infatuation, Inebriation and Intoxication of a Mughal King', *Mangalore Today*, 10 January 2019, https://tinyurl.com/yc3uwnk6, accessed 4 December 2025.

32. Tom Verde, 'Mallika V: Nur Jahan', *AramcoWorld*, 26 October 2016, https://tinyurl.com/55xmk4x7, accessed 4 December 2025.
33. Henry Beveridge (ed.), *The Tuzuk-i-Jahangiri; or, Memoirs of Jahangir*, Alexander Rogers (trans.), London Royal Asiatic Society, 1909–14.
34. Edna M. Rawlings, *William Fremlen of India: The Story of a 17th Century Merchant*, 1994.
35. Oleg Cherne, 'Sufism and Wine', *Code de Vino*, n.d., https://tinyurl.com/2nx3r9vw, accessed 4 December 2025.

## 5. Colonial Capers: Spirits of Empire

1. Blake Smith, 'When a Greek God Brought Wine to India', *The Wire,* 18 November 2017, https://tinyurl.com/2faaatd6, accessed 20 November 2025.
2. Vikram Doctor, 'Tracing the History of Madeira: From Portugal to India', *The Economic Times*, 15 June 2014, https://tinyurl.com/rkxu9uvx, accessed 4 December 2025.
3. Ibid.
4. Lucile H. Brockway, *Science and Colonial Expansion: The Role of the British Royal Botanic Gardens*, Yale University Press, 2002.
5. Armin Zimmermann, 'Punch, Toddy, Grog & Co. – Part 4: Punch – An Indian Drink', *Bar-Vademecum*, 15 August 2021, https://tinyurl.com/4xdz8yd7, 4 December 2025.

6. Peter Mundy, *The Travels of Peter Mundy in Europe and Asia*, Vol. 2, FB&C Limited, 2018.
7. Ibid.
8. Erica Wald, *Vice in the Barracks: Medicine, the Military and the Making of Colonial India* (1780–1868), Palgrave Macmillan, 2014, pp. xii, 273.
9. William Howard Russel, *My Diary in India 1858–59*, Routledge, 1860.
10. Jean-Baptiste Tavernier, *Travels in India, Vol. 1*, William Crooke (ed.), Oxford University Press, 1925.
11. Sam Goodman, 'Spaces of Intemperance & the British Raj 1860–1920', *The Journal of Imperial and Commonwealth History*, vol. 48, no. 4, pp. 591–618, https://doi.org/10.1080/03086534.2020.1741840.
12. Harald Fischer-Tiné, '"The Drinking Habits of Our Countrymen": European Alcohol Consumption and Colonial Power in British India', *Journal of Imperial and Commonwealth History*, vol. 40, no. 3, 2012, pp. 383–408, https://doi.org/10.1080/03086534.2012.71 2379.
13. Prasun Chatterjee, 'The Lives of Alcohol in Pre-colonial India', *The Medieval History Journal*, vol. 8, no. 1, 2005, pp. 189–225.
14. https://tinyurl.com/46m7e9kd, accessed 4 December 2025.
15. Kevin A. Morrison, 'Mr Samuel Smith, M.P.', *Charity and Philanthropy in Nineteenth-Century Britain, Routledge*, 2025.

16. 'East India (Abkari Department)', *Hansard 1803–2005*, 30 April 1899, vol. 335, cc817–77, https://tinyurl.com/46m7e9kd, accessed on 12 December 2025.
17. Nitin Varma, 'Producing Tea Coolies?: Work, Life and Protest in the Colonial Tea Plantations of Assam, 1830s–1920s, Dissertation, Humboldt-Universität zu Berlin, 1 December 2011, https://tinyurl.com/mvjjtpu9, accessed 12 December 2025; Surojit Baruah, 'Spread of Country Liquor in the Late Colonial Assam (1905–1947), *Proceedings of the Indian History Congress*, vol. 63, 2002, pp. 995–1003.
18. David Hardiman, 'From Custom to Crime: The Politics of Drinking in Colonial South Gujarat', *Subaltern Studies IV: Writings on South Asian History and Society*, Ranajit Guha (ed.), Oxford University Press, 1985, pp. 165–228.
19. Henry Hobbs, *John Barleycorn Bahadur: Old Time Taverns in India*, Mackenzie Lyall & Company, 1943.
20. Ibid.

## 6. Interdiction and Indulgence: Independence and Beyond

1. Personal interview.
2. 'Scotch Whisky: India Outdrinks France as Top Buyer by Volume', *BBC News*, 13 February 2023, https://tinyurl.com/yc7a22xk, accessed 4 December 2025.

3. David M. Fahey and Padma Manian, 'Poverty and Purification: The Politics of Gandhi's Campaign for Prohibition', *The Historian*, Vol. 67, No. 3, 2005, pp. 489–508, https://tinyurl.com/4t4rned8, accessed 26 November 2025.
4. *Bansi Lal, MLA (Ex Chief Minister)* vs *State of Haryana and Others*, No. 18625 of 2001, 30 January 2003, https://tinyurl.com/2tvbuakx, accessed 4 December 2025.
5. Debasree Purkayastha, 'Camphor in a Ring of Fire', *The Hindu,* 16 November 2021, https://tinyurl.com/yc4fyfdx, accessed 20 November 2025.
6. International Institute for Population Sciences (IIPS) and ICF, *National Family Health Survey: India 2019–21*, Vol. 1, Mumbai, 2021.
7. Personal interview.
8. Future Market Insights, *India Alcohol Market: Analysis and Growth Projections for India's Alcohol Industry Business*, 2025, https://tinyurl.com/4r63cu2n, accessed 26 November 2025.
9. 'Bottoms Up! India Outdrinks Key Global Markets in Growth, Whisky Leads the Way', *Economic Times*, 6 November 2025, https://tinyurl.com/2hs6jez5, accessed 20 November 2025.
10. Sagar Malviya, 'Scotch Meets Match; Local Single Malts Win Hearts', *The Economic Times*, 1 June 2025, https://tinyurl.com/jna5z99z, accessed 26 November 2025.

11. 'Indian Drinking Habits/Trends 2025', *Aristham,* 16 October 2024, https://tinyurl.com/2jje8euy, accessed 20 November 2025.